Mugsar International School Debating Competition

"What kind of a student is a student who does not know Sumerian?"

SUMERIAN CUNEIFORM

ENGLISH DICTIONARY

MUGSAR

ED. PETER & TARA HOGAN

12013CT

"Selfishness lasts a day
Civilization endures forever"
- Unknown Sumerian Scribe c.7000CT

To

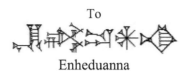

Enheduanna

7715-7750CT

The earliest known author and poet was female

(and most likely black)

"Something has been created that no one has created before."

MUGSAR

Published '2017 Peter Hogan
ISBN: 978-1-52206-200-4

Reproduction / Contact

Use proper attribution where relevant, see the Reference section. It's all part of the unearthing process, Civilization Time, belongs to all of us, especially when the subject matter is the displaced first one – can you just see that black *Kiengi* designing that first tablet some 5400 years ago.

Oh, and don't forget the all important step 1... Write or tattoo your name in cuneiform! This is ours:

DUB.SAR
(tablet . write)
1207E + 122AC
{scribe}

Peter Hogan
Mugsar Founder
amazon.com/author/peterhogan
mugsarsumerian.com
sumeriancuneiformdictionary@gmail.com
PO Box 1 Potts Point NSW 1335 Australia

Check Top Google Ranking

We all know the name of the game in life, especially with marketing to consumers and careers, is encapsulated by the simple, but critical phrase, "How to really impress someone."

Now, like the Sumerians conveyed their concepts with images on tablets, the Mugsar conveys it with the modernday equivalent, digital images. One of our key markteting taglines is based on the fact that the Mugsar is the ultimate way to impress someone, and that such an audacious statement actually has credibility, and can be tested with Google.

Imagine someone glances over your shoulder, and don't see some brainless gameapp, instead they see you exploring the Mugsar.

How to really impress someone

So where do you think it ranks on Google Images - remembering this is not an iPhone8 promotion, we have no $zillion advertising campaign like Apple.

Test it for yourself, enter the keywords "how to really impress someone" in **Google Images**.

To check Mugsar's top Google ranking: Google images

how to really impress someone

..

CONTENTS

Foreword

This is the updated authorized Mugsar Collector's Edition for Amazon Paperback Direct Publishing by Mugsar Founder and Editor Peter Hogan. (Beware of unauthorized pirated copies). The Mugsar Sumerian Cuneiform English Dictionary, the only standalone one in the world for the founders of Western Civilization, was first published 7 October 2013 on Internet Archive and australiansofarabia.wordpress.com also academia.edu

Through buying the Mugsar Collector's Edition (MCE) you will be supporting the development of the Mugsar and helping to get the Sumerians back to their rightful position on education curriculums ahead of the Establishment's dictated hierarchy of courses, essentially "groups that plagiarized the Sumerians".

In return, not only do you get the altruistic satisfaction of seeing the Mugsar gaining ground in Amazon and Google rankings, you also get, for all time, a free listing on the **Mugsar Immortal Benefactors Register** (MIBR). Simply email your purchase details, and if your really want to be an active benefactor, post a "Verified Purchase" review on Amazon and/or on social media just include something like "Just bought my #MugsarSumerian dictionary - my favorite cuneiform sign is 12217 LUGAL king".

If we ever get to the point of an IPO all your financial support will be convertible to stock options, dollar for dollar. And as one of the early supporters you and/or your kid will be highly favored when it comes to paid positions, like Mugsar VP Marketing for your region.

More details and customized options for benefactors at the New Mugsar Sumerian Cuneiform Dictionary Home (mugsarsumerian.com) – Immortalizer.

Peter Hogan
Mugsar Founder
16viii12017CT

..

Book Description

The Mugsar Sumerian Cuneiform English Dictionary is the only standalone one for the founders of Western Civilization in the world. And talk about nifty:

⟩ The unique "Mugsar 4-Way"

1. unicode 2. sign 3. lemma 4. translation

All on one screen. At elite university sites it's all over the place. None give unicodes and their translations are superficial / computer generated.

⟩ The real nifty part, the "Mugsar QuickFinder" Index

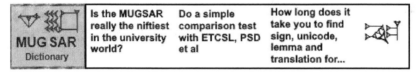

| MUG SAR Dictionary | Is the MUGSAR really the niftiest in the university world? | Do a simple comparison test with ETCSL, PSD et al | How long does it take you to find sign, unicode, lemma and translation for... | |

The first great civilization (fl c. 6600CT - 8000CT) were the Sumerians - "ki.en.gi", who were black ('saĝ gig.ga') to boot! For the enlightened Sumer is aptly termed the 'cradle of civilization'.

Much has been plagiarized from them without due attribution, not just the wheel, writing, law, but even true etymologies - the real origins of so many English words like 'abzu' = abyss, not to mention 'shekel', the Hebrew term for money -- some would have us believe that everything starts with the Greeks and Romans, world champion plagiarizers themselves. Our libraries may as well forget the non-fiction / history section - just put it all under fiction. How some can relegate this great civilization to what's conjured by terms like "ancient" and "BC". It's not going backwards, they come first at about 6600CT.

The Greeks were closer to Sumer
than Sydney to Perth or
New York to Los Angeles
... and they (and others) didn't
pick up anything over 3000 years?!

Tablet1

Inspiration for all this came out of not being able to find a Sumerian cuneiform sign list with unicode, lemma and translation. There are some amazing dedicated websites and books produced by some amazing academes {missing fragment} ...from the experience of living in Japan and studying *kan-ji*, it became obvious that you have to have the logogram, reading and translation all together. Just reading and translation is useless. And now of course linking everything is the unicode – see our unique 'Mugsar 4-Way', an example: ..

Inanna and the Seven Cosmic Powers of her Loincloth
u$_4$-/ba nin-ĝu$_{10}$ an\ mu-un-niĝin$_2$-na-ta
Once, my dear lady heaven roamed around,

cpd	cpd	1222C	1202D	cpd closeup
ud-ba	nin	- ĝu$_{10}$	an\	/mu-un-niĝin$_2$-na-ta\
Once 12313 UD day + 12040 BA open halve	lady, mistress 122A9 MUG + 12306 TUG$_2$ garment	'dear one' Determ. / honor.	heaven	roamed around 1222C MU name + 12326 UN (KALAM = Sumer) + 121B8 niĝin$_2$ encircle + 1223E NA incense + 122EB TA much

Some well funded universities like Oxford's Faculty of Oriental Studies, ETCSL et al have everything separated, don't give unicodes at all, and for the sign they link off to PSD (University of Pennsylvania) where it is often not clear which is the relevant one. And their translations are superficial, probably computer generated. When you work with the actual cuneiform signs, rather than just impotent readings using our boring English phonetic script, you start to see that the scribes were not just telling a story, but literally painting the scene.

When we start going deeper than such misleading translations it becomes very revealing. It's not just that to the chagrin of some, that the Sumerians keep referring to themselves as black, there's a sign in particular that clearly tells us that the very first professors, scholars, experts, master craftsman, the ones who could write and teach, were black...

Inana's black braided hair
7400CT

$1222A = MI / gig_2 = black$

...and 'um-mi-a' is not just of a more recent period of only 4000 years ago (Ur III) it goes way back to over 5000 years ago (ED IIIb) [a good 2000 years before the Greeks et al]:

ummia [EXPERT] (142x: ED IIIb, Old Akkadian, Ur III

expert, master craftsman 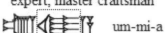 um-mi-a	Not just the Sumerians calling themselves black, the first professors are BLACK!	
7000CT/5000ya	7500CT/4500ya	8000CT/4000ya
14	110	18

PSD

..

diĝir [DEITY] (1837x: ED IIIb, Old Akkadian, Lagash II, Ur III
"deity, god, goddess" **The gods are black too!**

[1]		diĝir (dingir)
[2]		dim$_3$-me-er (ES)
[3]		dim$_3$-me$_8$-er (ES)
[4]		dim$_3$-mi-ir (ES)
[5]		di-me$_2$-er (ES) PSD

..

Gilgamesh, the hero of oldest written epic is also black

BIL.GA.MEŠ (Sumerian: Bilgamesh [cf.
Billjim!]; Akkad.: Gilgamesh) [1224B BIL$_2$ burnt + 120B5 GA young
(bull) + 12229 mes (meš) black hero (next on the sign list is the more
common black sign 1222A MI; and 1207E dub able to
write = power connotation)]

And not only were the first scholars black, the earliest known author
and poet was female (and most likely black), Enheduanna.

..

It's even more bewildering when you see someone like Jeremy Black ('1951-
'2004) founder of ETCSL, publish *Literature of Ancient Sumer* but leaves out
the actual cuneiform. Starting with the Introduction (see Google Books) he
adeptly covers the nuances using the awesome 9x6cm tablet containing 16
lines of *Nertal's Axe* story, encouraging the reader to begin to feel how
enchanting Sumerian cuneiform is. Yet he sticks solely to what he calls "our
Latin alphabet" (didn't it come west via the Phoenicians [Lebanon], as in the
phonetic alphabet!) in giving Sumerian readings and transliteration. Straight
off he could have shown he was going to be totally faithful. Why not show
us the beautiful picture of the magical axe, which when we go hunting for it
on his own ETCSL baby (c573.4) we find (hazin,
see 12154). What a shame. Jeremy must have known the signs intimately,
and could have told us so much about his personal findings on their
evolution and little things to look for in the pictures. Likewise with *The
Oxford Handbook of Cuneiform Culture* – with a title that highlights the
word cuneiform, yet way less than 1% actually shows signs. Really there
should have been at least a chapter about the 300 most common Sumerian

cuneiform. Nope, just some 800 pages of English phonetic script. And incredibly expensive. Yet you can find much of it around the Net (see Google Books for starters) and some fair dinkum cuneophiles share their contributions for free, like Frans van Koppen's Chapter 7 *The Scribe of the Flood Story and His Circle* at academia.edu (a backup of the Mugsar is there too).

..

The scribes who invented writing 5000 years ago clearly had no inhibitions about the basis for the design of their cuneiform, nor should we bowdlerize [etym.: Thomas Bowdler expurgated William Shakespeare (aka Edward de Vere) '1822] for hypocritical luddites / puritans who are still happy to plagiarize the technology revolution started by the Sumerians, and it may well have been the inspiration for the whole style ~ cunei.form = cuneus writing.

Scratching and dragging a pointed stylus would not have been near as effective and enduring for us to be able to read now. And it can be no coincidence that the Sumerian apotheosis of 'woman' through the cuneus -

shaped **V** sign has come down to us as the first letter of vagina, a fundamental example of our *True Etymology* campaign.

..

To top it off, at long last, for the many frustrated cuneophiles out there, comes the nifty Mugsar QuickFinder Index. Can you find an elite university that nifty?

Oh, and if any nuts were looking for evidence that these first great civilizations got some help from aliens ...well, your first glance at the arrangement of many signs sure reminds one of spaceships, docking

modules, rocket thruster exhausts – take a look at 12217 LUGAL King he's in a spaceship man! As you would expect for the King of the Sumerians / "Kings of the Earthlings".

Seriously though, enduring Sumerian picture script on tablets offers us a lot more than say Greek phonetic writing on papyrus (much of it disintegrated almost immediately). One might first say that for starters the Greeks were much more intellectual. But how much of the basics were plagiarized from the Sumerians.

With the tablets we have a conduit, like electrons through a main circuit travelling at the speed of light straight back 5000 years ago. Analogous to astronomers and their powerful telescopes peering back into the evolution of galaxies (now there's an aptly interesting *True Etymology* – see 120F2 GAL big) and the universe. The pictures the scribes have transmitted on those tablets impress a profound insight into exactly how the people of the first civilization were thinking. Even with only a basic familiarity with the meanings of the logograms, it can be like watching timeshifted live video. Much more fascinating than the most expensive Steven Speilberg blockbuster but then what's a movie without a scriptwriter, and we're talking about the very first writers ever, who put down the motifs of Gilgamesh and Inanna.

Stop a moment and think about it. Put the huge amount of time in perspective. In that time many cultures did not develop writing at all, some had it and lost it. When plagio-religio somehow began to dominate the Romans the West was plunged into the Dark Ages, ironically only a bunch of monks were allowed to rehash one group of stories with a flood story, etc., plagiarized from guess where. Writing has really only started to make a comeback in the last few hundred years after the Renaissance / Enlightenment (even Guillem Shaksper's Stratford daughter couldn't write). That's less than 10% of the timeline back to the Sumerians.

So at the next party you can say "I like movies" or "I'm studying a second language, French..." or you can say, "I'm a collaborator on the **MUGSAR** ...

a nifty little ⟨Tablet⟩ (they had it a bit before Steve Jobs!) we are developing so anyone can watch the Sumerians walking around 5000 years ago..."

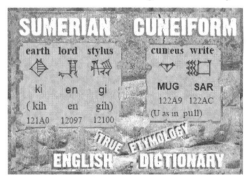

..

New MugsarSumerian Home

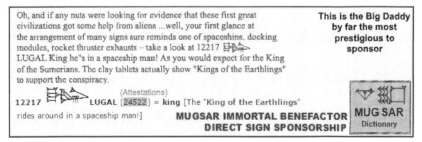

The New Mugsar Sumerian Cuneiform Dictionary home is at **mugsarsumerian.com** where you can also find customized options for benefactors, see Immortalizer (mugsarsumerian.com/immortalizer.htm)

..

Why Support the Mugsar?

What's in it for me, my family, my school, my business, my community?
Taking the high road, it's a major altruistic endeavor.
From a selfish viewpoint, it's a genuine shot at immortality.
To validate such a bold answer let's do a comparison.

Which has a better shot at Immortality: iPhone vs Mugsar?

You know the iPhone from the zillion dollar Apple advertising campaigns.
It's an apt comparison because founder Steve Jobs (11955-12011CT) is of the same generation, as is Microsoft's Bill Gates (b. 11955CT) to Mugsar Pete's (b. 11956CT), but he never ran into a Steve Wozniak or a Paul Allen, who were critical in the start of both enterprises.
The epochal Mugsar is the only standalone Sumerian Cuneiform Dictionary for the founders of 'education' in the world.
Compare its world ranking already with elite professors without $1 in support at **academia.edu** (considering too most of these professors get a $120K+ lifetime salary but few produce papers that students look at, where as there's Pete's Mugsar produced in stone cold poverty).

* 'THE' Professors average 131 followers study
(timeshighereducation.com/news/phd-students-run-professors-close-in-twitter-popularity-contest)

Ms Jordan's study, which was shared at a seminar hosted by the Society for Research into Higher Education last month, also sheds light on how academics use different types of social networks differently.

In contrast to the large networks found on Twitter, and the use of this site to exchange ideas with diffuse communities, academics tend to have far fewer followers on specialist websites such as Academia.edu and ResearchGate – an average of 68 each – and often use these platforms as a type of online business card.

Networks on these sites also tend to be more tightly clustered, with linkages between academics often representing face-to-face relationships built up through departments, institutions and research collaborations.

Professors have an average of 131 followers each, compared with 60 for lecturers and 68 for researchers. PhD students, in contrast, have an average of just 31 followers each.

[*Katy Jordan - PhD student, Open University] Chris Havergal 20Oct15
timeshighereducation.com/news/phd-students-run-professors..

..

Only the Mugsar rides the coattails of, and promotes 'Civilization Time' for all students in all cultures.

It constantly highlights the position of the Sumerians in CT to avoid the naivete of referring to them as 'ancient', and as a symbol that we are all part of its ascent - no cultural or class barriers, and so that users can see an unbroken timeline cf. the incumbent broken zero missing backwards sectarian year counting.

The Mugsar will become the defacto standard for every student in every school in the world to know Sumerian Cuneiform.

Can any other product realistically boast a market share that big?

We're not talking iPhones grabbing 30% of world market share, and wondering can they maintain it against Android et al.

Will the whole Apple corporation be even in existence in 1000* years? [*For the Mugsar we could easily add lots of zeros to the time frame but we'll keep the argument within a sporting chance for Apple.]

Can you even imagine how people will communicate in 1000 years, a chip implant or something direct to the brain?

Will a well run society's top educators think it reasonable to make sure students know Sumerian Cuneiform and how they founded 'education' to make Western Civilization possible in the first place. (Will they really be able to keep their jobs by only pushing the Romans and Greeks, like they got nothing from the Sumerians?)

Or will those students be browsing the Mugsar with those brain implants?

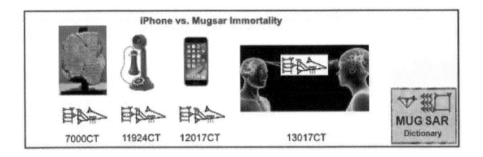

Which do you think has a better shot at growing market share, year in year out, decade in decade out, century in century out, millennia in millennia out – iPhone or Mugsar?

Which do you think has a better shot at immortality – iPhone or Mugsar?

Benefactors-Sponsors of Mugsar Sections-Signs

One day you will be gone.
Nobody will know you ever existed.
Why be forgotten?

Immortalize yourself, your family, your school, your business, your community by sponsoring the entire Mugsar, sections, like the nifty QuickFinder index, individual signs.

It's something like what happens in archaeology where a newly discovered dinosaur is named after a benefactor, like "**Anzu wyliei** – Chicken from Hell" named for the benefactor's grandson, Wylie J Tuttle.

Obviously signs would ha*f*ve different values, depending on special attributes. High value ones would be particularly prestigious, for example, the very first on the alpha-numeric unicode system:

12000 ⟙ A vowel; water… { ⬛ The Xxxxxx Family 12017CT}
[The icon used is niĝul, an everlasting possession;120FB niĝ$_2$ possession + 1230C ul distant time]

Heck, even dispossessed families like ours could be assigned some immortality pixels somewhere, including obscure variants that may still become more valuable for compound-making; and even turning graphics like the cover into a 10x10 pixel mosaic (aka image mapping) .
All plots would link to the official Mugsar Immortal Benefactor Register (MIBR).

Finder's Commission 80% !!!

There would be a whopping 80% Finder's Commission if the new MIB is found by an existing MIB. More details at the **Immortalizer** page.

Mugsar Worldwide Headquarters

Being the school/town that becomes the Mugar's wordwide headquarters could one day not only make you famous but also be an injection into the local economy, especially by creating jobs and hosting the MugsarFest (see below). All welcome. No candidate too small.

Whatever happens, it would be nice to think one day there will be a campus at the Mugsar Founders' Byron Bay Australia ancestral home, **BallyHogan** est. **'1882** - as close as possible to the mystical **sphinx-pyramid** conjuring **Hogans Bluff** (Picadilly Hill Rd Coopers Shoot NSW).

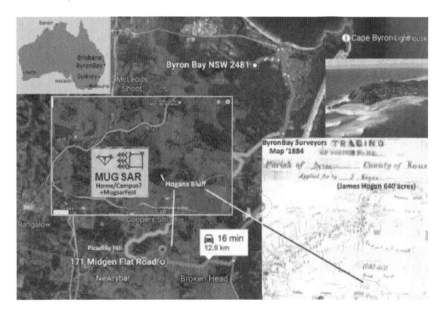

SUMERIAN CUNEIFORM DICTIONARY

Hogans Bluff on original BallyHogan '1882
looking east to Pacific Ocean from Picadilly Hill Rd
Lois Buckett Real Estate Byron Bay Echo

MugsarFest

Sales/auctions of signs; workshops – like how to write on clay; prizes for best clay tablet works, including replicas of famous Sumerian clay tablets, like the Gilgamesh Epic.
There would be 2 levels of MugsarFests:
1. MugsarFest International – a big annual event held to rival top film festivals hosted by the worldwide headquarters.
2. MugsarFest Fundraisers at the local level – meaning at any school, town, charity, not-for-profit. In areas of unemployment these could be setup to provide job experience or volunteer work, perhaps leading to paid positions. No registration or permission required, just go ahead and do it. If you make money, great. A bonus comes from geting new patrons to become Mugsar Immortal Benefactors and sponsor a sign back at the MugsarSumerian home which would garner a Finder's Commission, see above.

Mugsar Careers / Internships / Volunteers

There are going to be lots of opportunities. Let us know what you have to offer or be the first one to setup a local MugsarFest Fundraiser and make a name for yourself.

Mugsar World Tour / Guest Speaker / Video Conferencing / Personal Tuition

Pete, Mugsar Founder, will reciprocate your support in any way possible.

Merchandising

Mugsar Clay Tablets - more details will be at mugsarsumerian.com - there will be customized tablets for benefactors, see Immortalizer

Educational GameApp

The Mugsar GameApp will be a natural progression if we can find an altruistic programmer. It will make learning Sumerian Cuneiform fun, easy and of course, nifty. It will incorporate all kinds of exercises. For instance, scoring points depending on the time taken to find a particular sign, unicode, lemma, and translation.

Plan B - a PBL shows 'em all, and why education must change for the 121st Century It would be awesome if whiz kids nurtured at a PBL (Project Based Learning like at High Tech High San Diego) school pulled off the GameApp. Automatically making it internationally famous.

IPO

Every startup dreams of a successful IPO and cashing in stock options, especially a genuine epochal altruistic one that can give Menlo Park - Silicon Valley - Venture Capitalists something very rare in exchange, Immortality.
The idea is, every sponsorship dollar now would convert to stock options

later. So not only do you get longterm benefit, immortality, but also a bonus in the shortterm. How long? Dare we entertain an IPO within 10 years. Historically, looking back, which would have deserved an IPO more in the 121st century, Facebook or Mugsar?

Mugsar Foundation

Last but not least, one day when we stumble onto a big benefactor we will have a Mugsar Foundation with a Board of Trustees (with a blood descendant of the founder, of course) eternal guardianship to increase the chances of our shot at immortality.

Mugsar Chant

Oldest Education Proverb (c. 7000CT / 5000 ya)
dub-sar eme-gi nu-mu-un-zu-a a-na-am$_3$ nam-dub-sar
What kind of a student is a student who does not know Sumerian?

cpd	cpd	cpd closeup	cpd	cpd
dub-sar	eme-gi	nu-mu-un-zu-a	a-na-am$_3$	nam-dub-sar-ra-ni
scribe 1207E DUB tablet + 122AC SAR write	Sumerian language 12174 EME language + 12100 GI reed / write	not know (in all of Sumer) 12261 NU not + 1222C MU name + 12326 UN (KALAM / Sumer) + 1236A ZU know + 12000 A bemoan	what 12000 A bemoan + 1223E NA aux. + 1202D AN invoke the gods	scribe's craft 12246 NAM determined order; destiny + cpd DUBSAR scribe + 1228F RA (rah$_2$) [verb aux.] + 1224C NI come to pass

..
'education' true etymology = edub

Of course, the shame is not on the student, we all know where the social responsibility lies when we are talking about the oldest written language – the first schools, the founders of education (indeed, that word's *True*

Etymology is clearly edub, 3000 years before Latin plagio). So we can just as easily substitute, "What kind of teacher / professor / dean / principal / chancellor / school / university / education department director / culture..."

Youtube 9 sec video:
youtu.be/1l9gQndgt6Ae

How to use

The Main Listings follow same order as the standard cuneiform unicode (alpha-numeric) column after column (why didn't the powers that be just keep the codes sequentially all numeric?!). If you only have the sign try Major Lemma, then the QuickFinder Index.
First lemma (reading / syllable) after grapheme is usually the 'sign name', sometimes the Sumerian name as well, as are any other readings / aliases after that.
High resolution of logograms will come eventually, for now use ScriptSource (e.g. "unicode 120F6").

And the Mugsar is proudly, and primarily, a Sumerian dictionary of the first writers, not Akkadian, Babylonian nor Hittite ones. So we pretty much are only interested in lemma that go back to at least Ur III (8000CT / 4000ya). Nor lemma that have 0x attestations. Again there are some great lexicons around but they include a big chunk of this latter stuff, when plagiarizing the Sumerians was in full swing. And don't even show attestations, nor you know what... it's bad enough that there are no signs, but to think that much is not even Sterling-Sumerian, or rarely used, well.

You may notice with sign evolution, that it goes from the proto drawings to the cool Sumerian cuneiform, and then about 1000 years after them the fantastic pictures are lost through over simplification and the move to bland phonetic script. Who wants to look at that kind of dictionary.

Some may say the first writers are lacking more intellectual concepts. But maybe those can still come. There's two ways for them to still make it into Mugsar one day: 1) such cuneiform may eventually be unearthed 2) as we take in so many awesome signs gathered together on one *QF* screen (not java programmed all over the place – will PSD be as easy as the Mugsar to pass on to future generations via the Internet Archive?!) the more familiar we get with the way Sumerian (not Akkadian, Greek, Roman et al) scribes were thinking 4-5000 years ago, then you know what we could be capable of? If we can start thinking like a scribe, why shouldn't we be able to pick up the stylus, and carry on their work, by fusing any missing intellectual cuneiform, including rendering of new technology terms.

And so, that's why we are proudly snobs of Mugsar!

..

MAIN LISTINGS

MAJOR LEMMA

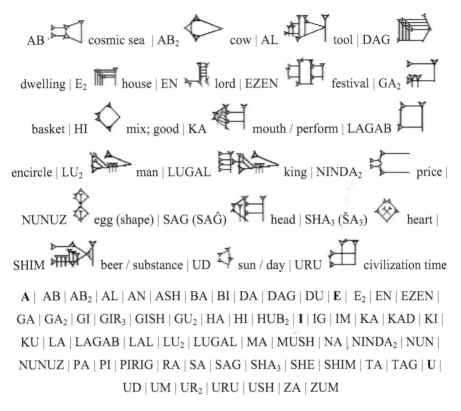

AB cosmic sea | AB₂ cow | AL tool | DAG dwelling | E₂ house | EN lord | EZEN festival | GA₂ basket | HI mix; good | KA mouth / perform | LAGAB encircle | LU₂ man | LUGAL king | NINDA₂ price | NUNUZ egg (shape) | SAG (SAĜ) head | SHA₃ (ŠA₃) heart | SHIM beer / substance | UD sun / day | URU civilization time

A | AB | AB₂ | AL | AN | ASH | BA | BI | DA | DAG | DU | E | E₂ | EN | EZEN | GA | GA₂ | GI | GIR₃ | GISH | GU₂ | HA | HI | HUB₂ | I | IG | IM | KA | KAD | KI | KU | LA | LAGAB | LAL | LU₂ | LUGAL | MA | MUSH | NA | NINDA₂ | NUN | NUNUZ | PA | PI | PIRIG | RA | SA | SAG | SHA₃ | SHE | SHIM | TA | TAG | U | UD | UM | UR₂ | URU | USH | ZA | ZUM

..

MAIN LISTINGS
Numeric Unicode & A-Z Lemma [914]

12000 𒀀 **A** [vowel; 2329x] = water (plural only) | (mû) (most often complimented with MEŠ) | progeny, heir; [110x] a cry of woe, bemoan, (sigh of) wonder, groan (aya) | dur₅, duru₅ [227x] = soft; wet, moist, damp; irrigated; fresh | { ⬭ The Xxxxxx Family 12017CT}

cpds 𒀀𒁲 ID₂, i₇ [1086x] = river, canal | determinative &id₂; river names

𒀀𒈾 a-na [566x] = what?; as much as [it takes] (math.) [~ + 1223E NA aux.]

𒀀𒀭 am₃ = [50x] to be [copula variant cf. 12228; 12000 A progeny + 1202D AN deity; True Etym. English 'am'] | šeĝ₃ (šeg₃) [70x] = to (fall as) dew; to rain; rain

𒀀𒁀 a-ba [326x] = who [12000 A progeny + 12040 BA share]

A Variants:

uQQ 𒀀𒀀 a-a (aya) [561x] = father | cf. 1201C 𒀀𒀀

12001 𒀀 A x A; 12002 𒀭 A x BAD; 12003 𒀀 A x GAN2 tenu;

12004 𒀀 A x HA | saḫ₇ (Borger zaḫ₃) [481x] = to disappear; to move away, withdraw; to stay away; lost; fugitive

12005 𒀀 A x IGI; 12006 𒀀 A x LAGAR gunu; 12007 𒀀 A x MUSH;
12008 𒀀 A x SAG

12009 𒀉 A₂ (á), ID, TI₈, IDUM= [6115x] arm /limb; labor; wing; horn; side; strength; wage; power | time | [Evol.: shoulder + arm] | cpd 𒀉 id-gurum (id-gur₂) [2026x] = ladle | 𒀉𒀭 AN, a₂-an [48x] = spadix (plant spike, erection)

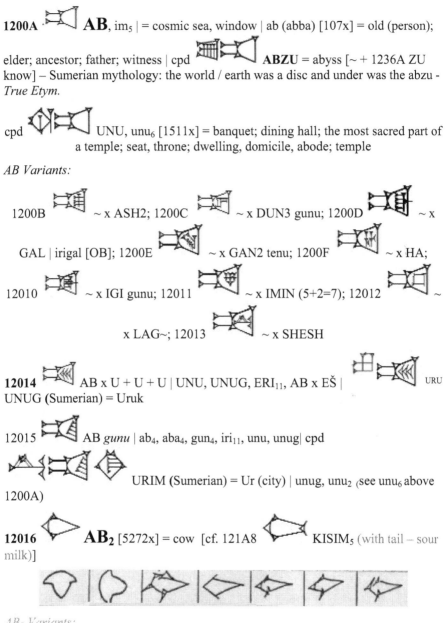

1200A **AB**, im$_5$ | = cosmic sea, window | ab (abba) [107x] = old (person); elder; ancestor; father; witness | cpd **ABZU** = abyss [~ + 1236A ZU know] – Sumerian mythology: the world / earth was a disc and under was the abzu - *True Etym.*

cpd UNU, unu$_6$ [1511x] = banquet; dining hall; the most sacred part of a temple; seat, throne; dwelling, domicile, abode; temple

AB Variants:

1200B ~ x ASH2; 1200C ~ x DUN3 gunu; 1200D ~ x

GAL | irigal [OB]; 1200E ~ x GAN2 tenu; 1200F ~ x HA;

12010 ~ x IGI gunu; 12011 ~ x IMIN (5+2=7); 12012 ~

x LAG~; 12013 ~ x SHESH

12014 AB x U + U + U | UNU, UNUG, ERI$_{11}$, AB x EŠ | URU UNUG (Sumerian) = Uruk

12015 AB *gunu* | ab$_4$, aba$_4$, gun$_4$, iri$_{11}$, unu, unug| cpd

URIM (Sumerian) = Ur (city) | unug, unu$_2$ (see unu$_6$ above 1200A)

12016 **AB$_2$** [5272x] = cow [cf. 121A8 KISIM$_5$ (with tail – sour milk)]

AB$_2$ Variants:

12017 ~ x BALAG;

12018 ~ x GAN2 tenu | šem₅ [14x] = a drum

12019 ~ x ME + EN;

1201A ~ x SHA3 | lipiš [40x] = inner body; heart; anger, rage | šem₃, ub₃
[15x] = a drum

1201B ~ x TAK4

1201C AD [36x] = father [cf. uQQ aya (561x)] | ad [26x] voice;
cry; noise | [13x] log; plank

cpd ad-da = father [~ + 12055 DA line (gen.)] | *True Etym.* "dad"

1201D AK (ag) [3643x] = to **do**; to make; to act, perform; to proceed,
proceeding (math.)

cpd im-ak-a-bi = revenge [1214E IM anger + 1201D AK
to do
+ 12000 A bemoan + 12049 BI open]

MU-AK = do (cooking) [1222C MU name, cook + 1201D AK do]

1201E AK x ERIN2 | me₃ [243x] = battle, combat

1201F AK x SHITA + GISH

12020 AL [744x] = hoe / hoeing, pickax [tool; CVNE = compound verb nominal element]

AL Variants:

12021 ~ x ~; 12022 ~ x DIM2; 12023 ~ x GISH;

12024 ~ x HA; 12025 ~ x KAD3; 12026 ~ x KI;

12027 ~ x SHE; 12028 ~ x USH

12029 ALAN, ALAM [399x] = statue, icon, form | (GUD/GUD).NA₂| cf.

1223F Nu₂ lay, bed

1202A ALEPH [reconstructed (first) sign => "A" ??; cf. HI sweet/good; ox (head)]

1202B AMAR [2771x] = young, youngster, son, descendant; calf / young bull, chick | zur | cpd amar-utu = MARDUK (bull calf of the sun god utu – northern hemisphere 12 day winter solstice celebration of his birthday, later plagarized by various cultures) [~ + 12313 utu sun]

1202C AMAR x SHE (ŠE) = sacrifice, ritual

1202D AN, DIĜIR (dingir) [1837x] = sky, god, goddess, deity, cosmic; heaven; upper; crown (of a tree) | determinative divine names &d; | plant spadix (spike) erection - see 12009

1202E AN/AN;

1202F AN x 3 | AN/AN.AN, mul [129x] = star; to shine, radiate (light); arrow; to radiate (branches) [Tara! (also in *sanskrit*)] | determinative &mul; stars / planets cpd mul-an [33x] = cosmic star [1202F MUL star + 1202D AN cosmic]

12030 AN + NAGA OPP. AN + NAGA; 12031 AN + NAGA sq

12032 ANSHE / anše = [2957x] donkey, equid (hoofed mammals) | DUR$_3$, DUSU$_2$ | ANŠE+NUN+NA = mule | ANŠE+KUR+RA = horse | determinative donkey/horse names &ance;

12033 APIN, ^{GIŠ}apin (uru$_4$) [741x] = (seed) plow | uru$_4$ [359x] = sow, cultivate | ^{LÚ}engar = farmer | àbsin = furrow (long shallow trench)

12034 ARAD, ÌR (ir$_3$), níta, nitaḫ = [269x] slave, servant

12035 ARAD$_2$ (ir$_{11}$) x KUR = [3028x] slave, servant [from the hinterland / mountain tribes]

[PLM] Jaritz #668 '(male) slave'. It is normally read as arad2 but it also reads ge24 for *gi24 which simply means 'male'; and that the meaning 'male' is derived from *gix, phallus, making gi24 *gî24.

12036 ARKAB | arkab$_2$ = [0x!] bird or bat | argab (GAR-IB)

12037 ASAL$_2$ | asal$_x$ = [0x!] poplar tree [PSD aliases: asar$_2$ ašar$_2$ (A.TU.GABA.LIŠ)]

12038 ASH / AŠ [191x] = **1** ("1" one numeric) | dili [227x] = single, unique, sole; alone

12039 ASH ZIDA tenu; 1203A ASH KABA tenu

1203B  ~/~ TUG2/TUG2 TUG2/TUG2 PAP

1203C ASHx3, ESH / **EŠ** = **3** ("3" three numeric)

1203D   ASH/~/~ +-ing ~/~/~ | KASH / kaš$_2$ (kas) = beer, alcohol [1344x] cf 12049

1203E   ASH$_2$ (út), aš$_2$ = curse [51x]

1203F   ASHGAB / AŠGAB [631x] = leather-worker

12040   BA = [839x] split; to divide into shares, share, halve, to allot; porridge; [26x] animal, marine creature; [11x] open, thresh | [19x] tool (cpd reed stylus)

[PLM]   central line demarcating the gluteal cleft of the buttocks [True Etym. buttocks], with the line extending below as a tail, to make its position on the anatomy clear cf. Inanna L116 [Jaritz #5]

cpd   su$_8$-ba (ES) [25x] = shepherd

ba-ni-in-dug$_4$-ga = more violent threshing about [12040 BA threshing + 1224C NI quiver + 12154 IN = abuse, rape + 12157 dug4 / KA = perform + 120B5 GA suckling, hold]

ba-ni-in-su-ub-ba = kissing [12040 BA thresh about + 1224C NI quiver+ 12154 IN = abuse, rape + 122E2 SU submerge, flesh + 12312 UB praise, ruin]

12041   BAD, BE | [109x] remote; to open, undo | SUMUN, SUN = LÚ+BAD = lord | MUNUS+BAD = lady | ÚŠ = death, destruction | reed stylus ?? cf. 12357   uš$_2$ = die, kill; blood | cf. 12300   TIL

12042   BAG$_3$?? = qqq [numeric ??; ba-ga ?? | pag, bag, bak, pak, HU, 12137]

12043   BAHAR$_2$ [315x] = potter

12044 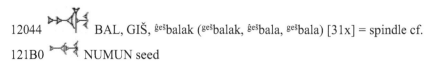 BAL, GIŠ, ᵍᵉˢbalak (ᵍᵉˢbalak, ᵍᵉˢbala, ᵍᵉˢbala) [31x] = spindle cf.

121B0 NUMUN seed

cpd balbale (bal-bal-e) [34x] = literary subscript [~x2 + 1208A e speak]

12045 BAL/BAL

12046 BALAG [154x], DUB₂ = harp, large drum (instrument)

12047 BAR [2579x] = outside, (other) side; behind; outer form, outer; fleece; outsider, strange; back, shoulder; liver; because of; to set aside; to cut open, slit, split | HALF; LÚ+MÁŠDA = poor man | MAŠD+TAB+BA = TWIN cf 12226

12048 BARA₂, barag = [423x] ruler, king; dais, seat; [52x] sack; a part of an animal's body; [7x] mix

12049 BI / PI, KASH / kaš [13889x] = beer; alcoholic drink | determinative ᵏᵃᶜ; alcohol | (* *True Etym. bi => beer*); open [also 1203D]

1204A ~ x A

1204B ~ x GAR | bappir₃ [385x] = an ingredient in beer-making

1204C ~ x IGI gunu

1204D BU, GID₂ = [2252x] long, length | bur₁₂ (bu) = to tear [189x; verb]

1204E ~/~ AB; 1204F ~/~ UN; 12050
~ +-ing ~

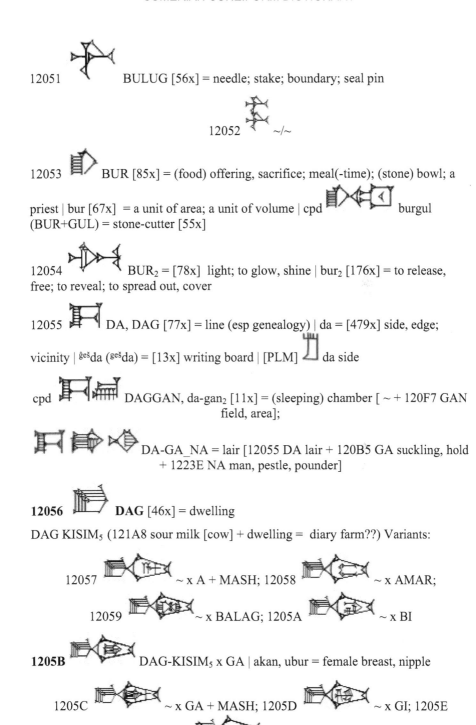

12051   BULUG [56x] = needle; stake; boundary; seal pin

12052   ~/~

12053   BUR [85x] = (food) offering, sacrifice; meal(-time); (stone) bowl; a

priest | bur [67x] = a unit of area; a unit of volume | cpd   burgul
(BUR+GUL) = stone-cutter [55x]

12054   BUR₂ = [78x] light; to glow, shine | bur₂ [176x] = to release,
free; to reveal; to spread out, cover

12055   DA, DAG [77x] = line (esp genealogy) | da = [479x] side, edge;

vicinity | ᵍᵉˢda (ᵍᵉˢda) = [13x] writing board | [PLM]   da side

cpd   DAGGAN, da-gan₂ [11x] = (sleeping) chamber [~ + 120F7 GAN
                    field, area];

DA-GA_NA = lair [12055 DA lair + 120B5 GA suckling, hold
            + 1223E NA man, pestle, pounder]

12056   **DAG** [46x] = dwelling

DAG KISIM₅ (121A8 sour milk [cow] + dwelling = diary farm??) Variants:

12057   ~ x A + MASH; 12058   ~ x AMAR;

12059   ~ x BALAG; 1205A   ~ x BI

1205B   DAG-KISIM₅ x GA | akan, ubur = female breast, nipple

1205C   ~ x GA + MASH; 1205D   ~ x GI; 1205E

~ xGIR₂

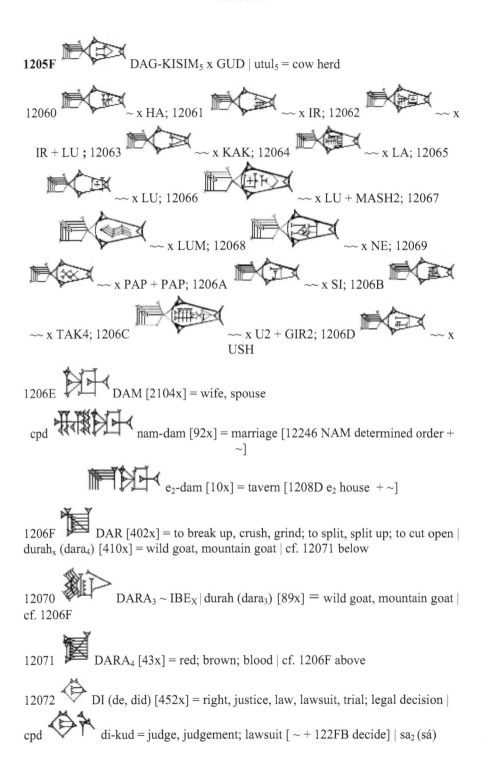

1205F DAG-KISIM₅ x GUD | utul₅ = cow herd

12060 ~ x HA; 12061 ~ x IR; 12062 ~ x

IR + LU ; 12063 ~~ x KAK; 12064 ~~ x LA; 12065

~~ x LU; 12066 ~~ x LU + MASH2; 12067

~~ x LUM; 12068 ~~ x NE; 12069

~~ x PAP + PAP; 1206A ~~ x SI; 1206B

~~ x TAK4; 1206C ~~ x U2 + GIR2; 1206D ~~ x
USH

1206E DAM [2104x] = wife, spouse

cpd nam-dam [92x] = marriage [12246 NAM determined order +
~]

e₂-dam [10x] = tavern [1208D e₂ house + ~]

1206F DAR [402x] = to break up, crush, grind; to split, split up; to cut open |
durahₓ (dara₄) [410x] = wild goat, mountain goat | cf. 12071 below

12070 DARA₃ ~ IBEₓ | durah (dara₃) [89x] = wild goat, mountain goat |
cf. 1206F

12071 DARA₄ [43x] = red; brown; blood | cf. 1206F above

12072 DI (de, did) [452x] = right, justice, law, lawsuit, trial; legal decision |

cpd di-kud = judge, judgement; lawsuit [~ + 122FB decide] | sa₂ (sá)

[452x] = to equal, compare, compete, be equal to, rival; [91x] to tie (shoes); [46x] advice, counsel; resolution, intelligence | salim, silim [228x] = well-being; healthy, prosperity; completeness, favourable | syll.: ti$_4$

12073 DIB, DAB = GRASP | LU, UDU = sheep [cf 121FB]

12074 DIM [38x] = post, pillar, pole; binding, knot, bond; plant

12075 DIM x SHE / ŠE, DIM x KUR | MUN [427x] = salt; to be brackish; older ??

12076 DIM$_2$ [2109x] = to create, make, manufacture; to replace?; to bring forth?

12077 DIN [1x UNMNG – PSD: unknown/ED IIIb/Nippur...] cf. compound suffix - chariot, vegetable

12078 DIN KASKAL U *gunu* DISH

12079 DISH [5x!] = 1 ("1" one numeric) | GEŠ$_2$ [92x] = 60 sixty;| DIŠ (*gè*), GIŠ$_2$, NIGIDA

1207A DU [5868x] gin, ra$_2$, ri$_6$, ĝen (gen) = **to go** / come; [2789x] = to go; to flow | de$_6$ [1794x] / tum$_2$ [10x behind tum$_3$ 134x] = to bring / carry | GUB = stand

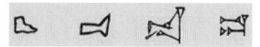

cpd e$_3$ (UD-DU) [1850x] = to leave, to go out; to thread, hang on a string; to remove, take away; to bring out; to enter; to bring in; to raise, rear (a child); to sow; to rave; to winnow; to measure (grain) roughly (with a stick); to rent [12313 UD sun + ~]

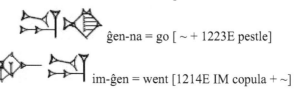

ĝen-na = go [~ + 1223E pestle]

im-ĝen = went [1214E IM copula + ~]

a-ra2 [4046x] = times (with numbers, multiplication); ways; way; omen; step (math.) [12000 A progeny + ~]

1207B DU/DU; 1207C DU *gunu*

1207D DU *sheshig* / *šešis*, gir₅, KASH / kaš₄ (kas₄) [1089x] = runner, trotter, messenger; to run

1207E DUB [1183x] = (clay) **tablet**, document | kišib₃ kishib₃ [17468xxx!] = cylinder seal, sealed tablet

[PLM] Jaritz #239 '(brick/tablet) mold', and is recorded to mean 'clay tablet', which is simply a 'molded loaf' put to an intellectual rather than a constructional use; dub also recorded to read dubb(-)a (for *dûppâ), which would represent 'molded (thing)' = 'tablet/brick'. Sumerian *dûp is also recorded for the meaning 'heap/pile up, spread out mud to make bricks'

cf. 12229 mes (meš₃), kišib black hero; 1231D UM reed (stylus?) stem

cpds:

dubsar [11320x] = scribe [1207E DUB tablet + 122AC SAR write] | *True Etym.*: English 'dub' (to name; give higher standing; replace script / sound)

eduba (e₂-dub) = education, school (Literature of Ancient Sumer, Jeremy Black, xxiv [Google Books]) | *True Etym.*: *edu*-cation [1208D e₂ house + ~]

gi-dub-ba = reed tablet stylus [12100 GI reed stem + 1207E DUB tablet + 12040 BA divide tool]

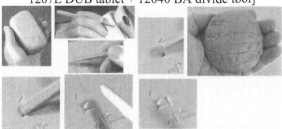

How to write on clay

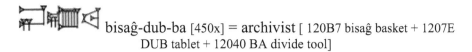 bisaĝ-dub-ba [450x] = archivist [120B7 bisaĝ basket + 1207E DUB tablet + 12040 BA divide tool]

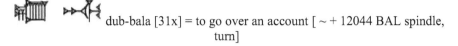 dub-bala [31x] = to go over an account [~ + 12044 BAL spindle, turn]

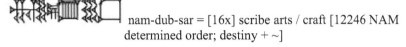 nam-dub-sar = [16x] scribe arts / craft [12246 NAM determined order; destiny + ~]

 nam-dub-sar-ra-ni = do. [+ verb aux.]

 e₂-dub-ba-a = scribe school [1208D e₂ school, house + 1207E DUB tablet + 12040 BA allot, share + 12000 water, progeny]

1207F   DUB x ESH2

12080   DUB₂ [186x] = to tremble, make tremble; to push away, down; to smash, abolish

12081   DUG [3196x] dugₓ(BI), BI x A = (clay) pot; a unit of liquid capacity | determinative vessels &dug;

12082   DUGUD [124x] = heavy, important

12083   DUH [556x] / DUḪ, DU, du₈ [2369x] = bake, to release, loose, loosen, undo, strip off; to spread out mud to make bricks; to caulk (filler, seal) TUḪ, DU₈, GAB | GABA = breast | cf. 120EE same sign GABA = copy; equal

cpd   mu-un-du₈-du₈ = stripped, made naked [1222C name, phallus + 12326 (KALAM = Sumer) + 120EE (/12083) du₈ (GABA) x2 strip off; spread; breast; equal [*NB double emphasis on strip / ravage*]]

12084   DUN [32x] = to dig

12085   DUN3, GIN₂, TUN₃ = cover | cpd saĝ-DUN₃ [447x] = land recorder; du₅-mu = apprentice (ES) [after 12309 dumu]

12086 DUN3 *gunu* | gig_4 (gin_2) [18136x] = unit of weight, shekel (see 122BA 'SHE'); a unit of area; a unit of volume | gel / kel, aga_3

cpd aga_3-kar_2 [5x] = conqueror [~ + uQQ kar_2 insult, blow up, light]

12087 DUN_3 *gunu gunu*

12088 DUN_4, DUL_4, $ŠUDUN_3$, $ŠUDUL_3$, UR *gunû šešig*, MIR*šešig* = yoke | mir (mer) [347x] = north wind; north; storm

12089 DUR_2 [98x] = rump rump, butt-ocks; defile, cleft [cpd suffix

e.g. wooden ledger board] | cf. 121AA

cpd dur_2-bi-$še_3$ = rump [12089 rump + 12049 BI open + 12365 $še_3$ string (cf. loincloth)]

1208A E [vowel; 399x] = to speak | perfect plural and imperfect stem of 'dug'; princely | interjection marker; fear, aura

1208B E x PAP

1208C E/E NUN/NUN

1208D ![E2 sign] **E₂** [13124x] = house, household; temple; station (of the moon)?; room; house-lot; estate | determinative &e₂; buildings / rooms names

cpd ![É.GAL sign] É.GAL = palace [~ + 120F2 GAL big]

![e-a-ni sign] e-a-ni = temple [~ + aux a-ni: "12000 A wonder + 1224C NI timelessness"]

E₂ Variants:

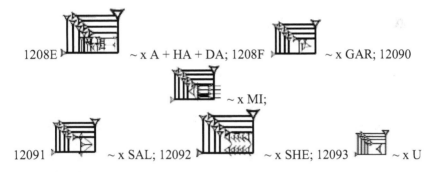

1208E ~ x A + HA + DA; 1208F ~ x GAR; 12090

~ x MI;

12091 ~ x SAL; 12092 ~ x SHE; 12093 ~ x U

12094 ![sign] EDIN / EDEN, bir₄ = steppe, open country; back [*True Etymology Dictionary*: 2000 years before religio Eden myths; note also Eridu] |

![Subir sign] Subir

12095  EGIR, eĝir (egir, eĝer) [393x] = back, rear; after; estate, inheritence; again

12096 ![EL sign] EL, SIKIL [457x] = pure | cf. 122DB ![SI sign] SI = horn [cuneus + horny = pure]

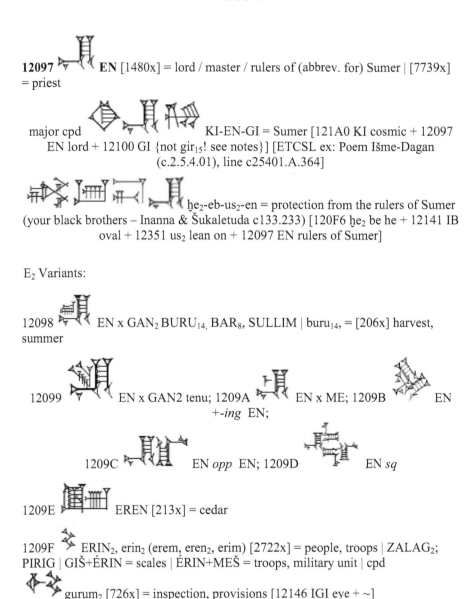

12097 EN [1480x] = lord / master / rulers of (abbrev. for) Sumer | [7739x] = priest

major cpd KI-EN-GI = Sumer [121A0 KI cosmic + 12097 EN lord + 12100 GI {not gir₁₅! see notes}] [ETCSL ex: Poem Išme-Dagan (c.2.5.4.01), line c25401.A.364]

he₂-eb-us₂-en = protection from the rulers of Sumer (your black brothers – Inanna & Šukaletuda c133.233) [120F6 he₂ be he + 12141 IB oval + 12351 us₂ lean on + 12097 EN rulers of Sumer]

E₂ Variants:

12098 EN x GAN₂ BURU₁₄, BAR₈, SULLIM | buru₁₄, = [206x] harvest, summer

12099 EN x GAN2 tenu; 1209A EN x ME; 1209B EN +-*ing* EN;

1209C EN *opp* EN; 1209D EN *sq*

1209E EREN [213x] = cedar

1209F ERIN₂, erin₂ (erem, eren₂, erim) [2722x] = people, troops | ZALAG₂; PIRIG | GIŠ+ÉRIN = scales | ÉRIN+MEŠ = troops, military unit | cpd

gurum₂ [726x] = inspection, provisions [12146 IGI eye + ~]

120A0 ESH₂ (EŠ ~ bà), gir₁₅ [7x! little as used] = native, local | cf. 1222A

ĝi₆ [7223x] = black ~ giving ki.en.gi ...Seems like some elites (incl those that control *Wakipedia*!) don't want to emphasize ki.en.<u>gi</u> = black Sumerians (are smarter because 'the reed stylus is mightier than the sword', see 12100 gi) -- they use instead non-Sumerian, little used (see notes), Babylonian 120A0 gir subscript

number **15** no less, which is really 'flour' 12365 zi₃ [7223x!] which such types,

incl. University of Pennsylvania's PSD relegates / obscures in italics as

..

[12401] eš₆ = "3" [numeric list]

120A1 **EZEN** (EZEM) [1136x] = festival; walled area?? | IZIN, KEŠDA | šir₃, sir₃ [150x] = sing, song, epic

EZEN Variants:

120A2 ~ x A; 120A3 ~ x A + LAL; 120A4 ~ x A + LAL x LAL; 120A5 ~ x AN

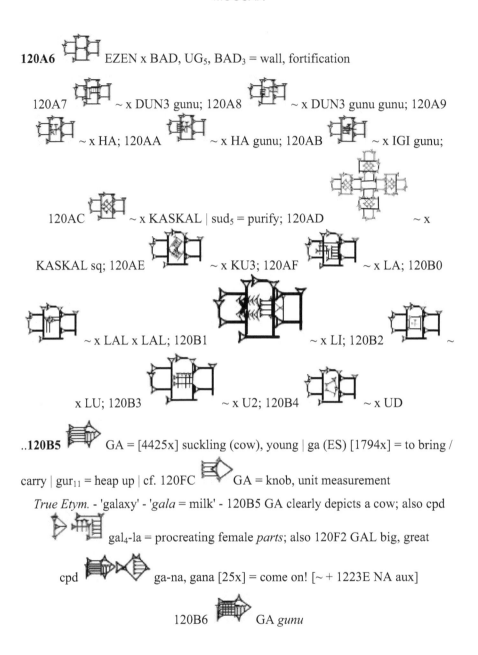

120A6 EZEN x BAD, UG₅, BAD₃ = wall, fortification

120A7 ~ x DUN3 gunu; 120A8 ~ x DUN3 gunu gunu; 120A9

~ x HA; 120AA ~ x HA gunu; 120AB ~ x IGI gunu;

120AC ~ x KASKAL | sud₅ = purify; 120AD   ~ x

KASKAL sq; 120AE ~ x KU3; 120AF ~ x LA; 120B0

~ x LAL x LAL; 120B1 ~ x LI; 120B2 ~

x LU; 120B3 ~ x U2; 120B4 ~ x UD

..120B5 GA = [4425x] suckling (cow), young | ga (ES) [1794x] = to bring /

carry | gur₁₁ = heap up | cf. 120FC GA = knob, unit measurement

True Etym. - 'galaxy' - '*gala* = milk' - 120B5 GA clearly depicts a cow; also cpd

gal₄-la = procreating female *parts*; also 120F2 GAL big, great

cpd ga-na, gana [25x] = come on! [~ + 1223E NA aux]

120B6 GA *gunu*

120B7 GA₂ (ĝa₂ / gá), mal, bisag / bisaĝ [704x] (pisan) = basket | [208x]

place [#2 behind 120FB 2500x] | ĝa₂ (ga₂) [67x] = house | PLM: shallow dish; jaw?? [pregnant??]

GA₂ Variants:

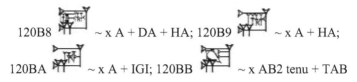

120B8 ~ x A + DA + HA; 120B9 ~ x A + HA;

120BA ~ x A + IGI; 120BB ~ x AB2 tenu + TAB

..

120BC GA₂ x AN, | ama = [863x] mother (goddess) | [PLM: maternal love - *True Etym.* cf. Latin *ama-re* / amor] | ama-lu | AMA-AN-MUŠ₃ | dagal [745x] = wide / broad; width, breadth

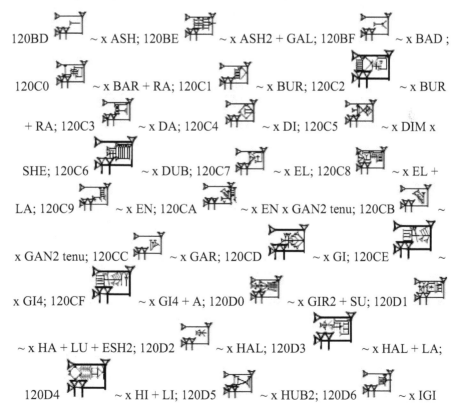

120BD ~ x ASH; 120BE ~ x ASH2 + GAL; 120BF ~ x BAD ;

120C0 ~ x BAR + RA; 120C1 ~ x BUR; 120C2 ~ x BUR

+ RA; 120C3 ~ x DA; 120C4 ~ x DI; 120C5 ~ x DIM x

SHE; 120C6 ~ x DUB; 120C7 ~ x EL; 120C8 ~ x EL +

LA; 120C9 ~ x EN; 120CA ~ x EN x GAN2 tenu; 120CB ~

x GAN2 tenu; 120CC ~ x GAR; 120CD ~ x GI; 120CE ~

x GI4; 120CF ~ x GI4 + A; 120D0 ~ x GIR2 + SU; 120D1

~ x HA + LU + ESH2; 120D2 ~ x HAL; 120D3 ~ x HAL + LA;

120D4 ~ x HI + LI; 120D5 ~ x HUB2; 120D6 ~ x IGI

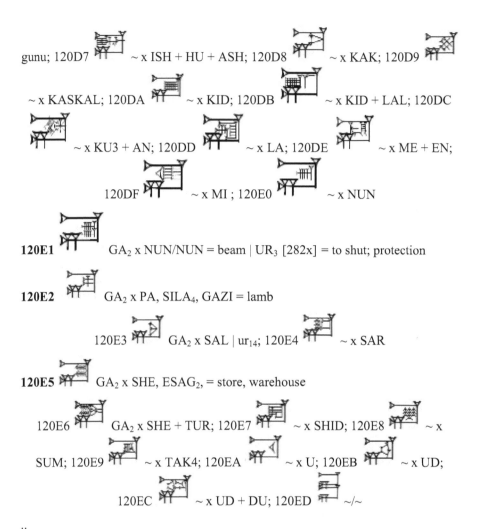

gunu; 120D7 ~ x ISH + HU + ASH; 120D8 ~ x KAK; 120D9

~ x KASKAL; 120DA ~ x KID; 120DB ~ x KID + LAL; 120DC

~ x KU3 + AN; 120DD ~ x LA; 120DE ~ x ME + EN;

120DF ~ x MI ; 120E0 ~ x NUN

120E1 GA₂ x NUN/NUN = beam | UR₃ [282x] = to shut; protection

120E2 GA₂ x PA, SILA₄, GAZI = lamb

120E3 GA₂ x SAL | ur₁₄; 120E4 ~ x SAR

120E5 GA₂ x SHE, ESAG₂, = store, warehouse

120E6 GA₂ x SHE + TUR; 120E7 ~ x SHID; 120E8 ~ x

SUM; 120E9 ~ x TAK4; 120EA ~ x U; 120EB ~ x UD;

120EC ~ x UD + DU; 120ED ~/~

..

120EE 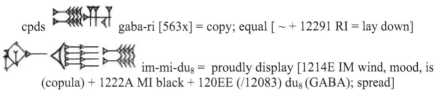 GABA, TUḪ, du₈ = [821x] breast, chest; frontier; [proudly display] | copy; equal | [3x] a designation of sheep | cf. 12083 same sign = release; spread

cpds  gaba-ri [563x] = copy; equal [~ + 12291 RI = lay down]

 im-mi-du₈ = proudly display [1214E IM wind, mood, is (copula) + 1222A MI black + 120EE (/12083) du₈ (GABA); spread]

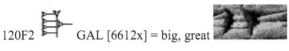 120EF GABA +-ing GABA

120F0  GAD (KAD) [633x] = linen, flax (plant fibre that is made into a thread and woven) cf.  MURUB₂

120F1 GAD/GAD GAR/GAR

120F2 GAL [6612x] = big, great

True Etym. - 'galaxy' [even if you take the '*gala* = milk' line, then we have 120B5 GA (sign clearly depicting a big cow) and cpd gal₄-la = procreating female *parts*

120F3 GAL GAD/GAD GAR/GAR

120F4 GALAM, SUKUD [227x] = height, altitude

120F5 GAM = down, below; [5x] pudenda | gurum, gur₂ [138x] = to bend, curve, wrap around; to bow; to roll up; to curb, restrain; to watch over | cpd id-gurum (id-gur₂) [2026x] = ladle

120F6 GAN / KAN [12x] = bear young; child-bearing [HO.GAN!] | he₂ (ḫe₂) [8x] = be (it / he / she) | be₂ [52x #2 behind e] = perfect plural and imperfect stem of 'dug'

cpd 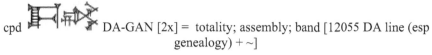 DA-GAN [2x] = totality; assembly; band [12055 DA line (esp genealogy) + ~]

ḫe₂-em = to be [~ + 1214E IM to be]

he₂-ĝal₂ [300x] = plenty [~ + 12145 ĝal₂ lay down]

PLM / True Etym. 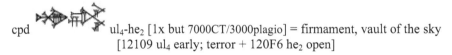 orig. reed jug over a waist with two legs', indicating a 'reed jug being carried, 'pointed-thing' = 'reed' [Jaritz #271] ... so can also be interpreted as 'carrying/storing a basket-like/womb'; and with this interpretation reads GAN, 'bear young'
From this Sumerian GAN / KAN cf. Greek kánna, 'reed, cane'... Latin canna, 'reed, cane, type of vessel', almost certainly the reverse process took place for the meaning 'reed, cane';... the source of canna ... 'jug'... 'pointed-thing-tool' = '(pointed, carrying) jug, amphora', seen in Greek kántharos, 'drinking cup' ... 'jug', seen clearly in Frankish cannada, 'jug' ... reeds were hollow, and could be used for jugs by merely cutting off a section sealed naturally at the bottom...

cpd  ul₄-he₂ [1x but 7000CT/3000plagio] = firmament, vault of the sky [12109 ul₄ early; terror + 120F6 he₂ open]

120F7 GAN2 / GAN₂, IKU = field, unit of area | determinative &iku; surface measurement

120F8 ~ tenu | kar₂ [55x] = to insult, slander | GAN2tenu-GAN2tenu, kar₂. kar₂ [52x] = to blow; to light up, shine; to rise

120F9 ~/~; 120FA ~ +-ing ~

..

120FB GAR, NINDA [11296x] = bread, pastry, baked, food – determinative

&ninda; bread / baked items | cf. less common 12252 NINDA₂ | ĝar (gar) [2505x] = place, to put, lay down; to give in place of something, replace; to posit (math.) | niĝ₂ (nig₂) [1641x] = thing, possesion; something | nindan (ninda) [149x] = pole; unit of length; 12 ?? | ŠA₂, | LIMMU = 4 | cf. 122E9

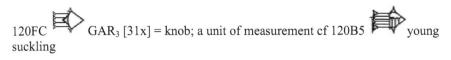

120FC GAR₃ [31x] = knob; a unit of measurement cf 120B5 young suckling

120FD GASHAN / GAŠAN = unit of area: one GAŠAN = 10 BÙRU (648000 M²) | U gunû, BUR₃ gunû = lady, mistress

120FE GESHTIN / ĝeštin (geštin) [796x] = vine; wine | GIŠ+DIN; giš.geštin

120FF ~ x KUR

[various] GE | 1230B ge₁₄; 12038 ge₁₅, saĝtak (santak); 12079 ge₃, saĝtak₄ (santak₄); 1203A ge₂₂, santak₂; 12039 ge₂₃, santak₃ = stylus cuneus; (piece of) writing, copy, exemplar, written; blow; wound | 122B9 | *True Etym.:* tack, small nail [saĝ ~ = 12295 headed (tack)]

12100 **GI** (*ge*) = [4900x] reed (stylus), [place of reeds / reed stylus => writing => knowledge => power (KI-EN-GI / Sumer – Tigris Euphrates delta ...see note)], cane [see True Etym. note], tube | gin₆ (gi, gen₆) [924x] = permanent; to confirm, establish (in legal contexts), verify; true; a quality designation; medium quality | ke₂ | determinative reed names &gi;

Many historians and anthropologists provide strong circumstantial evidence to posit that Iraq's Ma'dān (Marshland) people share very strong links to the ancient Sumerians - the most ancient inhabitants of southern Iraq... [Wik]
Studies show that Marshland people have a high concentration of Haplogroup J1 [mainly North Africa] for males.
See Genetic footprints of Sumerians in Iraq Marshlands (pdf).
Also see lively discussion here.
IAE, the reed stylus did come from the Marshlands:

gi-dub-ba
reed tablet stylus
[12100 GI reed stem + 1207E DUB tablet + 12040 BA divide tool]

Major cpds

 KI-EN-GI = Sumer [121A0 KI cosmic + 12097 EN lord +
12100 GI {not gir₁₅! see notes}]
[ETCSL ex: Poem Išme-Dagan (c.2.5.4.01), line c25401.A.364]

eme-gi [23x cf ~gir₁₅ 9x] = Sumerian language [12174 EME language
+ 12100 GI reed / write]

gi-dub-ba = reed tablet stylus [12100 GI reed stem +
1207E DUB tablet + 12040 BA divide tool]

12101 GI x E; 12102 ~ x U

12103 ~ +*ing* GI | GILIM, gi₁₆ = to lie across; to be entwined [together];
to entwine, twist; rope of twined reeds; to block; difficult to understand | gel / kel

cpd  gi₁₆-il = entwined (high up); foliage, forest

 gel-le-eĝ₃ (ES) = bad, evil; to forsake, forget; to destroy

[ES = emisal – female Sumerian]

12104 ![glyph] **GI₄** [1485x] = to turn, return; to go around; to change status; to return (with claims in a legal case); to go back (on an agreement)

cpd ![glyph] im-ma-ši-in-gi₄ = return leering eye [1214E IM mud, storm + 12220 MA approach + 12146 IGI watch + 12154 IN abuse + 12104 gi₄ return]

![glyph] gi₄-gi₄ = conversation (replies); jewellry; diviner (hidden knowledge)

 mu-na-ni-ib-gi₄-gi₄ = reply, advise, to and fro, conversation [1222C MU year, dear, name, son + 1223E NA pestle + 1224C NI comes to pass + 12141 IB oval + ~ x2; ETCSL c133.231]

![glyph] im-dab₆-gi₄-gi₄ = turning round and round [1214E IM mood, (copula) 1234F dab₆ go around, + 12104 gi₄ x2 turn, go around, return, change status; gi₄ x 2 therefore:'turn round and round' ??]

12105 ![glyph] ~/~; 12106 ![glyph] ~ +-ing ~

12107 ![glyph] GIDIM [45x] = ghost

12108 ![glyph] **GIR₂**, GIŠ, GÍR [198x] = knife, dagger, razor, sword | UL₄.GAL = sword

12109 ![glyph] ~ gunu | ul₄ [39x] = to hasten, (be) quick; early | ul₄ [12x] = terror | át=GÍR gunû [syll.]

PLM ![glyph] depicts a 'cocoon' => 'surround' [Jaritz #11]

1210A 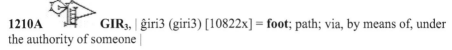 **GIR₃**, | ĝiri3 (giri3) [10822x] = **foot**; path; via, by means of, under the authority of someone |

cpd  huš (hush) [435x] = furious, angry; reddish, ruddy

1210B  ~ x A + IGI; 1210C ~ x GAN2 tenu; 1210D ~ x IGI;

1210E 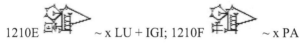 ~ x LU + IGI; 1210F ~ x PA

12110 GISAL | ᵍᵉˢĝisal (ᵍᵉˢĝisal) [19x] = rudder, oar; a roof part

12111 GISH, GIŠ, GEŠ = tree, wood | GIŠ.MI / GISSU = shade [ᵍⁱˢ = determinative &jic; before wooden objects]

12112 ~ +-ing ~; 12113 ~ x BAD

12114 ~ x TAK4; 12115 ~ tenu

12116 GU [1850x] = cord, net; unretted flax stalks; rump

12117  ~ +-ing ~

12118 GU₂, TIK | gun₂ (gu₂) / talent [5551x] = unit of weight (1 mina = 60 shekels. 1 talent = 60 mina); load; yield; rent, tax, tribute | [753x] = (river) bank; side; neck

12119 GU₂ x KAK, DUR = strip

1211A GU_2 x KAK x IGI *gunu*

1211B ~ x NUN; 1211C ~ x SAL + TUG2; 1211D ~

gunu

1211E GUD [17947x], gu_4 = bull, ox; cattle; calf; lion | determinative ^{&gud;}
cattle names

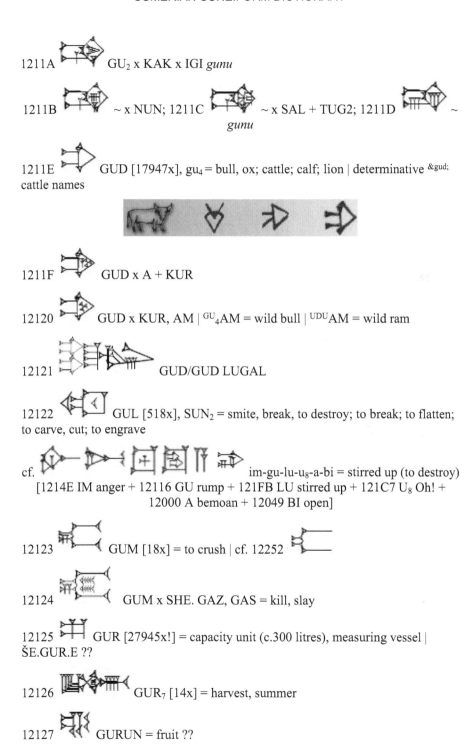

1211F GUD x A + KUR

12120 GUD x KUR, AM | ^{GU}$_4$AM = wild bull | ^{UDU}AM = wild ram

12121 GUD/GUD LUGAL

12122 GUL [518x], SUN_2 = smite, break, to destroy; to break; to flatten;
to carve, cut; to engrave

cf. im-gu-lu-u_8-a-bi = stirred up (to destroy)
[1214E IM anger + 12116 GU rump + 121FB LU stirred up + 121C7 U_8 Oh! +
12000 A bemoan + 12049 BI open]

12123 GUM [18x] = to crush | cf. 12252

12124 GUM x SHE. GAZ, GAS = kill, slay

12125 GUR [27945x!] = capacity unit (c.300 litres), measuring vessel |
ŠE.GUR.E ??

12126 GUR_7 [14x] = harvest, summer

12127 GURUN = fruit ??

12128 ⬚ GURUSH / ĝuruš (guruš) [9902x] = male, young adult male; able-bodied worker | cf. 12197 ⬚ powerful; rare

12129 ⬚ **HA** / **ḪA** | KU₆ = fish

1212A ⬚ ~ tenu; 1212B ⬚ ~ *gunu*

1212C ⬚ HAL = [55x] divide, deal out, distribute; to perform an extispicy [shaman fortune readings of organs of sacrificed animals]; to open; a secret; to pour away; to sieve; to slink, crawl away; a qualification of grain .. cpd HAL-HA ~ + 12129 fish | stick; disease; crotch

1212D ⬚ **HI** [2735x] hi [**pron.** *throaty* h] hi (ha₄), tí (dí), hi (he) = mix | dug₃ (du₁₀) [1587x] = **good**, good thing, goodness, sweet | dub₃ [55x] = knee | cf.

⬚ hul, hulu [13901x; uQQ] = bad

cpd ⬚ dug₃-ga = good [~ + 120B5 GA suckling, carry]

⬚ dub₃-nir = emit [1212D dub₃ knee + nir winnow]

⬚ hi(-iz)ˢᵃʳ [18x] = vegetable; lettuce [~ + 122AC ˢᴬᴿ determ. garden; see Lettuce Song in Erotica section]

HI Variants:

1212E ⬚ HI x ASH

1212F ⬡ HI x ASH2 (AŠ₂) | ur₅ [1215x] = interest-bearing loan; debt; requital, favour | ur₅ [190x] = he; that, this same; maid, female slave; one; corresponding (to one another); like (one another) | AR₃, KÍN, MUR | ḪAR = ring | ḪUR = thick | ḪUR₊SAG = mountain

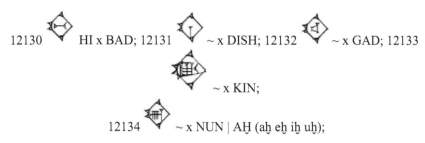

12130 HI x BAD; 12131 ~ x DISH; 12132 ~ x GAD; 12133 ~ x KIN;

12134 ~ x NUN | AḪ (aḫ eḫ iḫ uḫ);

12135 HI x (SHE) ŠE | dubur = horizon

12136 ~ x U

12137 HU (ḫu), mušen = bird | determinative &mucen; after bird names | bird laying egg, see 122DB

12138 HUB2 / ḪUB₂ [3x] = foot | HUBI [7x] = acrobat | left cf 1218F KAB, GAB₂, GUB₃ [CVNE = compound verb nominal element]

12139 HUB2 x AN; 1213A HUB2 x HAL; 1213B HUB2 x KASKAL;

1213C HUB2 x LISH; 1213D HUB2 x UD

..

1213E HUL₂ / ḪUL₂, hul₂ [347x] = joy .. cpd šag₄-hul₂ (ša₃-hul₂) [189x] = to be happy [122AE heart + ~] | ukuš₂ [39x] = cucumber

1213F I (vowel) | IA = "5" [five numeric] | [5x] hey! | [PLM] The ultimate basal meaning is 'set of eyes'; and from it, the prototypical 'pair', which, of course, is wholly arbitrary in view of 'two hands/legs, etc.'. Its use for 'many' is probably an extension of the idea of a naturally occurring 'set', regardless of the specific number: here, 'five (fingers)'...

cpd ⬚ i-bi$_2$ [50x behind igi 1082x] = eye, (prob esp) carved eye (for statues)

[1240A] ⬚ Í, IÁ, IA$_2$ = 5, 300; 12140 ⬚ I A

12141 ⬚ IB = [108x] oval; [0x] profession

12142 ⬚ **IDIM** = blocked, heavy, spring (underground water) ??

12143 ⬚ ~/~ BUR; 12144 ⬚ ~/~ sq

12145 ⬚ IG [88x] door | gal$_2$ / ĝal$_2$ [3954x] = to be (there, at hand, available); to exist; to put, place [/class ?? cf. mi-iq-tum (miqtum, mi-ĝal$_2$-tum) = social class], lay down; to have cf. copula

cpd ⬚ im-mi-ĝal$_2$ = classified [1214E IM mood, is (copula) + 1222A MI black (high) + 12145 ĝal$_2$ place, class]

12146 ⬚ **IGI** [1133x], ŠI, LIM = **eye**, vision, watch, notice; carved eye (for statues) | igi [3906x] = first, earlier; front; face | *True Etym.*: ig-no-re / ig-no-rant (not know/see) <= ig(i) + 12261 nu no .. IGI is an awesome cuneiform design by an unknown scribe (appearing on tablets over 5000 ya), one of our eReader Top 5, and the sound / reading too, obviously would have caught the eye of plariarists down the millennia; there's also something fishy about our "I" and "eye" (sound and arrangement of letters).

cpds

⬚ gurum$_2$ [726x] = inspection, provisions [~ + 1209F ERIN$_2$ people, troops]

pad$_3$ (reveal) cpds

⬚ pad$_3$ [2313x] = to find, discover; to name, nominate [~ + 12292 RU fall; throw]

⬚ mu-un-pad$_3$-da = revealed to the people [1222C MU name + 12326 UN (KALAM = Sumer) + ~ + 12055 DA writing board]

⬚ ga-ra-pad$_3$-pad$_3$ = like threshing grain will be revealed [120B5 GA bring + 1228F RA thresh + cpd pad$_3$ reveal x2] ga-mu-ni-pad$_3$ = find (esp revenge) [120B5 GA carry + 1222C MU name + 1224C NI in the end + pad$_3$ find]

nu-um-ma-ni-in-pad$_3$-de$_3$ = in all the lands could not find rapist (of Inanna) [12261 NU not + 1231D UM approach, disease + 12220 MA land; approach + 1224C NI in time+ 12154 IN abuse, rape (rapist + pad$_3$ find + 12248 de$_3$ carry]

uQQ HUL, HULU [13901x] = **bad,** to destroy; bad-smelling, maloderous; bad, evil; slight, lightweight; false; criminal, dishonest; enemy; to raid; to strike the eyes; blinker

12147 **IGI** DIB | U$_3$, Ù [6341x] = and; but; also | LIBIR = sleep, dream

cpd lu$_2$-u$_3$ = other; man and [121FD lu$_2$ man / him + 12147 u$_3$ and]

12148 IGI RI | ar [syll.]; 12149 ~/~ SHIR/SHIR UD/UD

1214A IGI *gunû*, SIG$_7$ = 10000 ; [62x] class of worker; [48x] to pluck hair or wool; trimmed, pruned

1214B IL = to be(come) high

1214C IL x GAN2 tenu

1214D IL$_2$ = [1362x] to raise, carry; (collect); [2x] worker; [0x] tax

1214E IM [680x] = clay, mud; tablet | determinative &im; made of clay | tumu, tum$_9$ [49x] = wind | determinative &tum9; winds | [48x] rain, storm (/ steaming anger) - [weather / mood] | [73x] em = to be (is / was) copula variant cf 12228 | ni$_2$

A curious development from EME [12174 tongue] 'voice-emit' = 'make a sound' is found in Jaritz #721, which depicts a 'sail with rigging' [cf. harbinger for antenna, radio signal] and reads *îm(i) (for *îm(i)); it means 'wind, storm-wind'; i.e. 'moaning (of the wind), pars pro toto' [a part (taken) for the whole]. Strong support for this analysis is furnished by another meaning attached to this sign: 'fear'; this is understandable for 'moaning' but not for simply 'wind' or 'storm(-wind)'. 'Moaning' has attracted the reading ni₂ [1224E ![sign]] 'be afraid', 'fear', which represents 'snivel-stative-like' = 'sniveling' = 'fear'.

cpd 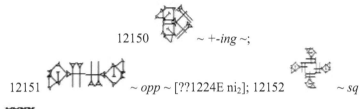 im-ma-ni-in-su-ub = kissing [1214E
IM storm + 12220 MA flow + 1224C NI quiver + 122E2 SU submerge, flesh + 12312 UB praise, ruin]

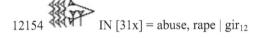 im-te-a-ni = himself / herself

1214F ![sign] IM x TAK4 | kid₇ [6x] = cut; break off; pinch off; scratch; demolish | cf. uQQ kid₂ = [1.] do., ~ [4.]

12150 ![sign] ~ +-ing ~;

12151 ![sign] ~ opp ~ [??1224E ni₂]; 12152 ![sign] ~ sq

12153 ![sign] **IMIN [31x] = "7"** (5+2) [seven numeric]

12154 ![sign] IN [31x] = abuse, rape | gir₁₂

cpd ![sign] hazin (urudha-zi-in / urudaha-zi-in) [128x] = axe [determ
1234F + 12129 HA fish + 12363 ZI raise + ~] See *Nergal's Axe* c573.4

12155 IR, GAG *gunû* = plead, ask; divinate; perfume ?? | DIG = soft [6x] |

cf. 1224C NI oil

12156 ISH (iš) [15x] = mountain; summer | kuš$_7$ (šuš$_3$) [1587x] = high official, bureaucrat, civil servant

12157 **KA** (gù) | KAG$_2$ [1329x] = **mouth** | du$_{11}$, dug$_4$ [3878x] = speak, talk, say; to order; to do, perform [cpd: 12351 + dug$_4$ = mating]; to negotiate | gu$_3$, kir$_4$ | inim (enim) [1329x] = word; matter (of affairs), thing | zú / zu$_2$ = teeth; plowshare (cutting edge) | kiri = nose

cpds: dug$_4$-ga-ĝu$_{10}$ = mating [12157 dug4 / KA = perform + 120B5 ga suckling, carry + 1222C ĝu$_{10}$ (MU) phallus, dear, name, son, year]

dug$_4$-ga-ni = mating

zu$_2$-kešda = compiler, organizer [12157 zu$_2$ cutting edge + 1219F kešda bind, organize]

"...The compiler of the tablets is Enheduana.
My king, something has been created that no one has created before."
[see Dedication]
etcsl.orinst.ox...c4801.543

KA Variants:

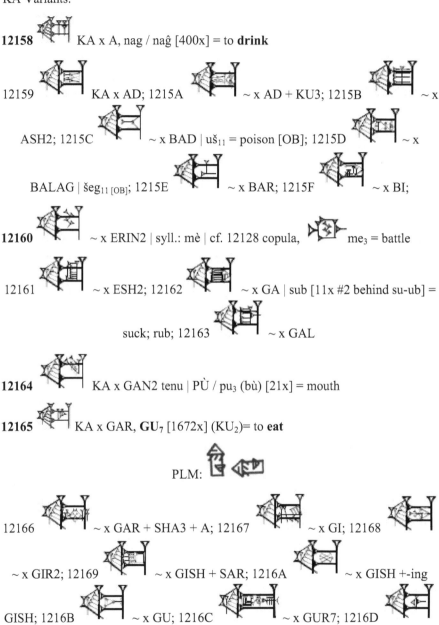

12158 KA x A, nag / naĝ [400x] = to **drink**

12159 KA x AD; 1215A ~ x AD + KU3; 1215B ~ x

ASH2; 1215C ~ x BAD | uš$_{11}$ = poison [OB]; 1215D ~ x

BALAG | šeg$_{11 [OB]}$; 1215E ~ x BAR; 1215F ~ x BI;

12160 ~ x ERIN2 | syll.: mè | cf. 12128 copula, me$_3$ = battle

12161 ~ x ESH2; 12162 ~ x GA | sub [11x #2 behind su-ub] =

suck; rub; 12163 ~ x GAL

12164 KA x GAN2 tenu | PÙ / pu$_3$ (bù) [21x] = mouth

12165 KA x GAR, **GU$_7$** [1672x] (KU$_2$)= to **eat**

PLM:

12166 ~ x GAR + SHA3 + A; 12167 ~ x GI; 12168

~ x GIR2; 12169 ~ x GISH + SAR; 1216A ~ x GISH +-ing

GISH; 1216B ~ x GU; 1216C ~ x GUR7; 1216D

~ x IGI

1216E KA x IM, BUN$_2$ = thunder, thunderstorm

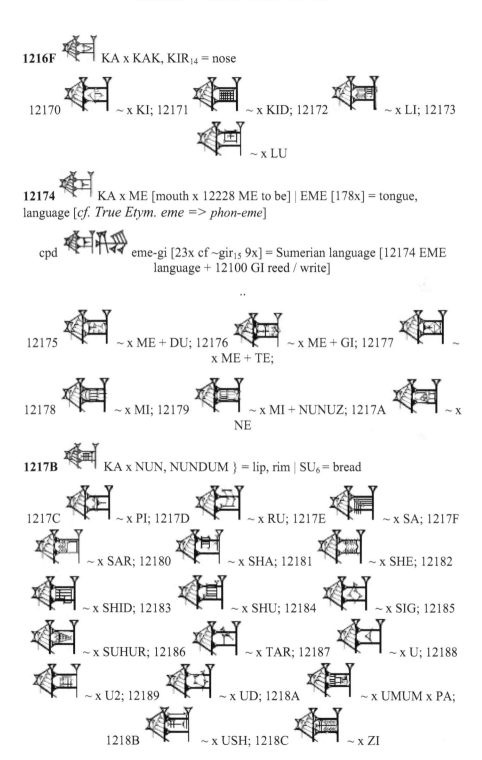

1216F KA x KAK, KIR₁₄ = nose

12170 ~ x KI; 12171 ~ x KID; 12172 ~ x LI; 12173

~ x LU

12174 KA x ME [mouth x 12228 ME to be] | EME [178x] = tongue, language [*cf. True Etym. eme => phon-eme*]

cpd eme-gi [23x cf ~gir₁₅ 9x] = Sumerian language [12174 EME language + 12100 GI reed / write]

..

12175 ~ x ME + DU; 12176 ~ x ME + GI; 12177 ~ x ME + TE;

12178 ~ x MI; 12179 ~ x MI + NUNUZ; 1217A ~ x NE

1217B KA x NUN, NUNDUM } = lip, rim | SU₆ = bread

1217C ~ x PI; 1217D ~ x RU; 1217E ~ x SA; 1217F

~ x SAR; 12180 ~ x SHA; 12181 ~ x SHE; 12182

~ x SHID; 12183 ~ x SHU; 12184 ~ x SIG; 12185

~ x SUHUR; 12186 ~ x TAR; 12187 ~ x U; 12188

~ x U2; 12189 ~ x UD; 1218A ~ x UMUM x PA;

1218B ~ x USH; 1218C ~ x ZI

..

1218D 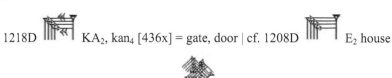 KA₂, kan₄ [436x] = gate, door | cf. 1208D KA_2, kan_4 ... E₂ house

1218E  KA₂ +-ing KA₂

1218F KAB, GAB₂, GUB₃, ḪUB₂ = left | cf. 12138

12190 kad₂ = qqq | "other letter" ?? | cf. 120FO KAD / GAD linen, flax;

122D9 šuš₂ cover

12191 kad₃ sed_x = qqq | "other letter" ?? |

12192 kad₄ = [1x!] fish; [9x] tie | peš₅ (pesh₅) [53x] = innards; to breathe; grandson; descendant; to give birth (to); pregnant; pregnancy; to gather; thick; wide | also uQQ peš [67x]

12193 KAD, kad₅ = [10x] to tie, gather; to itch, scratch; to weave a mat | banšur₃ (banshur) = table ??

12194  KAD5/KAD5

12195 KAK, gag [126x] = arrowhead; peg, nail | DU, DU₃ [cpd 12351 + ~ = mating], RU₂ [7061x] | GAG (dù) = to build, make do, perform

cpd 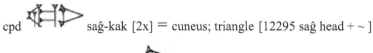 saĝ-kak [2x] = cuneus; triangle [12295 saĝ head + ~]

12196 KAK x IGI *gunu*

12197 ⊞ KAL, kalag = [102x] strong, powerful, mighty; to reinforce; to provide

for .. cpds ⊞⊞➤ kal-ga [2280x] ; kal-la [11x] | kal [389x] = rare, valuable |

cf. 12128 ⊞ young male

12198 ⊞ ~ x BAD; 12199  ~ +-ing ~

1219A ✦ KAM2, kám = prob. 'th' e.g. 15th day... [ordinal marker; can't find in
PSD et al – see waste of time below – penalty for not following most important rule
of 'Scribe School'] cf. "5" | change, desire ??

blood, pus, blister and pustule A.1. diš na ta-at-ti-kám ša kàš gig |
girNin-urta-kám Cuneiform Texts in the Metropolitan Museum of Art

and the third *nishu* of the balag gu₄-ud-nim (é)-kur-ra both have égi-re égi-re as the incipit. A tablet from
Nineveh, K 9342 + 10861 (joined by R. Borger; for K 10861 see Black, "Sumerian *Balag* Compositions,"
p. 47, and Cohen, *CLAM* 2, p. 469) has preserved the rest of an eršemma and the following caption:

Reverse

1. |ér-šèm-ma dim|girNin-urta-kám

2. |ér-šèm-ma n|ir-gal lú è-NE

Cuneiform Documents ed RH Sack:

62
WHM 1535

1) 3 BÁN ŠE.BAR *ina* ŠUK.ḪI.A *šá*
   Id*na-na-a*-KAM
2) A ⌈xx⌉ LÚ ⌈xx⌉ [. . .]
3) [. . .] IdAG-⌈ú-še-zib⌉
4) Id*na-na-a*⌈xxxx⌉
5) ⌈*ina* ŠUK.ḪI.A-*šú*⌉ I ÈR-*ia* GIŠ
6) ⌈*x*⌉ *ina* ŠUK.ḪI.A-*šú* Id*na-na-a*-KAM GIŠ
7) ITU.BÁR UD.15.KAM MU.⌈8⌉.KAM
8) dAG-NÍG.DU-ŠEŠ LUGAL TIN.⌈TIR.KI⌉

Translation
(Document concerning) eighteen qa of
barley, from the food allotment of Nanâ-
ēriš, son of [. . .] Nabû-⌈ušēzib⌉, Nanâ [. . .]
Ardija has received from his food allotment
(and) [. . .] (which) Nanâ-ēriš has received
from his food allotment. Month of Nisanu,
fifteenth day, ⌈eighth⌉ year of Nabû-
kudurri-uṣur, king of ⌈Babylon.⌉

UD. 15 .KAM MU .[8].KAM

day. 15. ?? year .[8]. ??

15th day, [8th] year of

UD=day; MU = year

Therefore, all this bloody trouble just to find that
KAM$_2$ is an ordinal marker (glyph/gloss) i.e. = **'th'**!!!

1219B KAM4 | zubi [6x] = watercourse, canal, irrigation

[120F8] kar$_2$ [55x] = to insult, slander | GAN2tenu- GAN2tenu,
kar$_2$. kar$_2$ [52x] = to blow; to light up, shine; to rise

1219C KASKAL [705x], KAS, RAŠ = way, road; journey, caravan |
DANNA = mile [distance]

1219D ~ LAGAB x U/LAGAB x U; 1219E ~/~ LAGAB x
U/LAGAB x U

1219F KESH2 / keš$_2$ (kešda) [853x] = to bind; gather; organize;
assemble; compile => {*computer tablet 5000 years later – and kešda looks like the
first computer mainframe, brought by aliens of course!*}

 zu$_2$-kešda = compiler, organizer [12157 zu$_2$ cutting edge + ~]

121A0 KI (*gi$_5$*) [32379xxx!] = cosmic (under)world (cf ABZU) earth, land,
place, ground, toward, country, lower, down below | determinative $^{\&ki;}$ after place
names |

 ki-ĝu$_{10}$-še$_3$ = designated place [121A0 KI place + 1222C
MU name, son + 12365 še$_3$ string]

121A1 KI x BAD; 121A2 KI x U; 121A3 KI x UD

121A4 KID, lil$_2$, ge$_2$ (*gé*), ke$_4$ = open field, steppe | ^{gi}kid [509x] = (reed)
mat | lil$_2$ [92x] = wind; ghost; female demon, Lilitu / Lilith of 'Bilgames
(Gilgamesh) and the Netherworld'

121A5 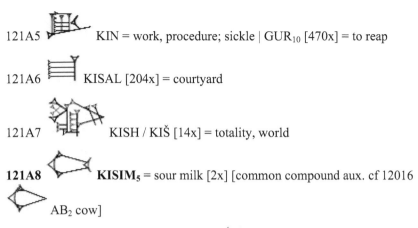 KIN = work, procedure; sickle | GUR$_{10}$ [470x] = to reap

121A6 KISAL [204x] = courtyard

121A7 KISH / KIŠ [14x] = totality, world

121A8 **KISIM$_5$** = sour milk [2x] [common compound aux. cf 12016

AB$_2$ cow]

121A9 ~/~

121AA KU = rump | DAB$_5$ [8723x] = to seize, take, hold; to bind; to envelop, overwhelm; to choose (by extispicy); to accept; to take charge of |

TUKUL, TUŠ = sit, seated | cf. 12089

121AB KU/HI x ASH2 KU/HI x ASH2

121AC KU$_3$, kug [1342x] = pure; [3875x] = metal, silver; bright, shiny | KUG+AN ~ AZAG = demon | KUG+GI ~ GUŠKIN = gold | ~ + BABBAR = silver

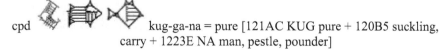

cpd kug-ga-na = pure [121AC KUG pure + 120B5 suckling, carry + 1223E NA man, pestle, pounder]

121AD 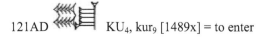 KU$_4$, kur$_9$ [1489x] = to enter

121AE  KU4

[122FB] KUD, ku5 [1111x] = to break off, deduct; to separate, cut off; to cut; to incise; to decide; to make clear

[12129] KU₆ = (fresh) fish | ᵏᵘ₆ = determinative &ku6; after names of fish

121AF KU7 / KU₇ [65x] = good; (to be) (honey-)sweet | KUD

121B0 KUL [59x] = to run | NUMUN [1219x] = seed cf. 12044 BAL spindle

cpd  šag₄.bala (ša₃-bal) [1016x] = procreate, to produce offspring
[122AE šag₄ heart + ~]

121B1 KUL *gunu*

121B2 KUN [225x] = tail; canal outlet

121B3 KUR [2494x] = mountain(s), land, country; underworld; east; easterner; east wind | determinative &kur; before mountains / countries

cpd  kur-kur-ra = mountains; lands [~ + 1228F RA aux.]

121B4 KUR opp KUR

121B5 KUSHU2 / KUŠU₂ = a paste; phlegm, mucus, sputum; foam, scum, cum; saliva, spittle; poison | creature, [12x] crab [the crabs!] [cuneus]

uQQ KUSHU / KUŠU, kuš₂ [149x] = tired, troubled

121B6 KWU318 = grass

121B7 [cuneiform] LA [65x] = bending over (rump); show, display; press; hang; supervise, check | [66x] a stand

PLM [cuneiform] bend, carry, press together, crease together, pinch [of buttocks]...practice pederasty, take advantage of a woman, cf. Sukaletuda's rape of Inanna L118 [Jaritz #968]; also Proto-Sumerian Halloran.

cpd lalamu | cf. 121F2 [cuneiform] la$_2$ | cpd [cuneiform] gal$_4$-la = behind

121B8 [cuneiform] **LAGAB** | niĝin$_2$ [214x] = encircle, go around | [116x] block, stump | GUR4 (KUR4) [133x] = thick, big, feel big | KILIB [256x] = total | LUGUD$_2$ = short, tight | gir$_8$ (kir$_3$) [2x!] = to break / pinch off | cpd
[cuneiform] mu-un-niĝin$_2$-na-ta = to roam around - see Mugsar 4-Way – Inanna112a

LAGAB Variants:

121B9 [cuneiform] LAGAB x A | SUG, AMBAR = swamp, marsh (encircled water) i.e. NÍĜINxA = AMBAR | BUGIN, BUNIN

121BA [cuneiform] ~ x A + DA + HA; 121BB [cuneiform] ~ x A + GAR; 121BC [cuneiform] ~ x A + LAL;

121BD [cuneiform] ~ x AL; 121BE [cuneiform] ~ x AN; 121BF [cuneiform] ~ x ASH ZIDA tenu

121C0 [cuneiform] LAGAB x BAD, GIGIR = cart

121C1 [cuneiform] ~ x BI; 121C2 [cuneiform] ~ x DAR; 121C3 [cuneiform] ~ x EN; 121C4 [cuneiform] ~ x GA; 121C5 [cuneiform] ~ x GAR; 121C6 [cuneiform] ~ x GUD;

121C7 [cuneiform] ~ x GUD + GUD | u$_8$ [4425x] = sheep, ewe; Oh!, (a soothing expression) | cpd nu-u$_8$-gig = priestess, high status woman, goddess / Inanna

121C8 [cuneiform] ~ x HA;

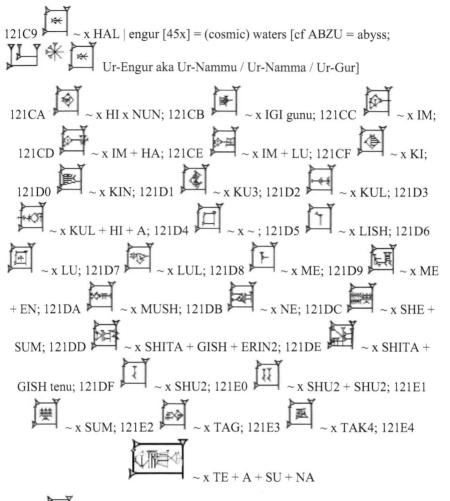

121C9 ~ x HAL | engur [45x] = (cosmic) waters [cf ABZU = abyss;

Ur-Engur aka Ur-Nammu / Ur-Namma / Ur-Gur]

121CA ~ x HI x NUN; 121CB ~ x IGI gunu; 121CC ~ x IM;

121CD ~ x IM + HA; 121CE ~ x IM + LU; 121CF ~ x KI;

121D0 ~ x KIN; 121D1 ~ x KU3; 121D2 ~ x KUL; 121D3

~ x KUL + HI + A; 121D4 ~ x ~ ; 121D5 ~ x LISH; 121D6

~ x LU; 121D7 ~ x LUL; 121D8 ~ x ME; 121D9 ~ x ME

+ EN; 121DA ~ x MUSH; 121DB ~ x NE; 121DC ~ x SHE +

SUM; 121DD ~ x SHITA + GISH + ERIN2; 121DE ~ x SHITA +

GISH tenu; 121DF ~ x SHU2; 121E0 ~ x SHU2 + SHU2; 121E1

~ x SUM; 121E2 ~ x TAG; 121E3 ~ x TAK4; 121E4

~ x TE + A + SU + NA

121E5 LAGAB x U | NÍĜINxBÙR (U) = pú (pu₂) [95x] = water well / hole, pit; depth (encircled area+hole) lower course, footing; cistern; fish pond; source (of river) | TÚL = source ?? | GÍGIR = wagon??

121E6 ~ x U + A; 121E7 ~ x U + U + U; 121E8 ~ x U2 + ASH;

121E9 ~ x UD; 121EA ~ x USH; 121EB ~ sq

cf. cpd SIPAD, sipa [2463x] = shepherd

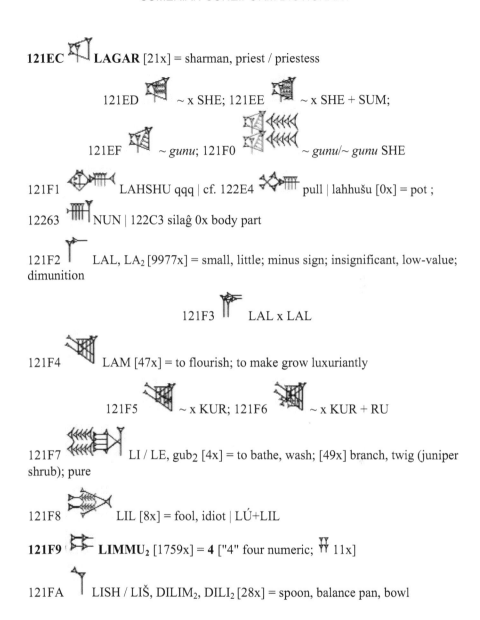

121EC LAGAR [21x] = sharman, priest / priestess

121ED ~ x SHE; 121EE ~ x SHE + SUM;

121EF ~ *gunu*; 121F0 ~ *gunu*/~ *gunu* SHE

121F1 LAHSHU qqq | cf. 122E4 pull | lahhušu [0x] = pot ;

12263 NUN | 122C3 silaĝ 0x body part

121F2 LAL, LA₂ [9977x] = small, little; minus sign; insignificant, low-value; dimunition

121F3 LAL x LAL

121F4 LAM [47x] = to flourish; to make grow luxuriantly

121F5 ~ x KUR; 121F6 ~ x KUR + RU

121F7 LI / LE, gub₂ [4x] = to bathe, wash; [49x] branch, twig (juniper shrub); pure

121F8 LIL [8x] = fool, idiot | LÚ+LIL

121F9 LIMMU₂ [1759x] = **4** ["4" four numeric; 11x]

121FA LISH / LIŠ, DILIM₂, DILI₂ [28x] = spoon, balance pan, bowl

121FB ⬛ LU | udu [28818xxx!] = sheep; [185x] abundant, to heap up; [130x] to disturb, stir up; to cover completely; to mix | DIB, DAB = grasp | [cf 12073

⬛] | determinative &udu; sheep / goats

cpd ⬛⬛ sipad (sipa) [2463x] = shepherd [1227A PA overseer + 121FB UDU sheep]

121FC ⬛ LU x BAD

121FD ⬛ **LU₂** [12429xxx!] = man (him); ruler *[alien spaceships!]*; person; who(m), which; (s)he who, that which; of; | determinative &lu2; before male stuff

LU₂ Variants:

121FE ⬛ ~ x AL ; 121FF ⬛ ~ x BAD; **12200** ⬛ ~ x ESH2;

12201 ⬛ ~ x ESH2 tenu;

12202 ⬛ ~ x GAN2 tenu | šaĝa (šaga) [6x] = a wronged person; slain; afflicted, oppressed

12203 ⬛ ~ x HI x BAD; 12204 ⬛ ~ x IM; 12205 ⬛ ~ x KAD2;

12206 ⬛ ~ x KAD3; 12207 ⬛ ~ x KAD3 + ASH; 12208 ⬛ ~ x KI; 12209 ⬛ ~ x LA + ASH; **1220A** ⬛ ~ x LAGAB; 1220B ⬛ ~ x ME + EN; 1220C ⬛ ~ x NE; 1220D ⬛ ~ x NU; 1220E ⬛ ~ x SI + ASH; 1220F ⬛ ~ x SIK2 + BU; 12210 ⬛ ~ x TUG2; 12211 ⬛ ~ tenu ; 12212 ⬛ ~ +-*ing* ~; 12213 ⬛ ~ *opp* ~; 12214 ⬛ ~ *sq*; 12215 ⬛ ~ *sheshig*

..

12216 LU$_3$ [18x] = to disturb, stir up; to cover completely; to mix

12217 **LUGAL** [24522xxx!] = **king** [The "King of the Earthlings" rides around in a spaceship man!]

True Etym.: 12217 LUGAL is made from 121FD LU$_2$ man + 120F2

GAL big => big man => king (sometimes scribes reverse signs - see Foxvog) cf. Latin *leg-is*; and lu/ru interchangeability => rugal => English 'regal', Latin *regalis*

LUGAL Variants:

12218 ~/~; 12219 *sheshig* ~ opp ~; 1221A ~

1221B LUH, **LUH, LAH**$_3$, sukkal [3469x] = secretary, civil servant, bureaucrat, official - *True Etym.:* sukkal => civil | luh [164x] = to clean, wash

1221C LUL [133x] = false, criminal | NAR = song / musician ??

1221D LUM [107x] = full, replete, satisfied (with); grown (tall); to fruit; fructified; to shine

1221E LUM/LUM; 1221F LUM/LUM GAR/GAR

12220 MA = [169x] (come in to) land (like bird; fly in), approach; go, flow (phallus, come), fig tree, house [?? secondary in each]

12221 MA x TAK4

12222 MA, gunu / *gunû* HAŠHUR / HASHHUR = apple (tree)

12223 MA2 / MA$_2$ [5559x] = ship, boat

12224 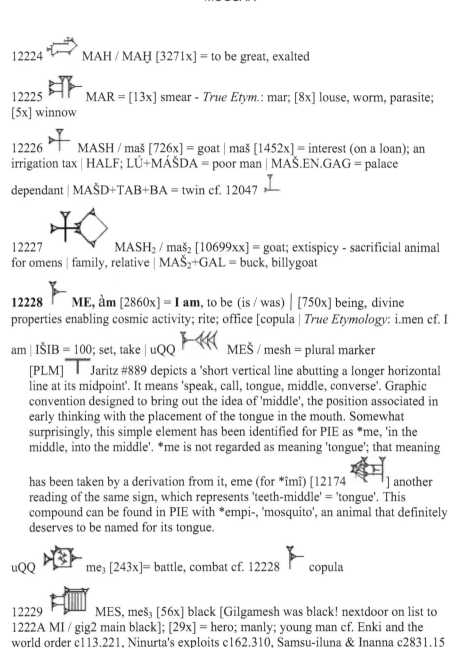 MAH / MAḪ [3271x] = to be great, exalted

12225 MAR = [13x] smear - *True Etym.*: mar; [8x] louse, worm, parasite; [5x] winnow

12226 MASH / maš [726x] = goat | maš [1452x] = interest (on a loan); an irrigation tax | HALF; LÚ+MÁŠDA = poor man | MAŠ.EN.GAG = palace

dependant | MAŠD+TAB+BA = twin cf. 12047

12227 MASH₂ / maš₂ [10699xx] = goat; extispicy - sacrificial animal for omens | family, relative | MAŠ₂+GAL = buck, billygoat

12228 ME, **àm** [2860x] = **I am**, to be (is / was) | [750x] being, divine properties enabling cosmic activity; rite; office [copula | *True Etymology*: i.men cf. I

am | IŠIB = 100; set, take | uQQ MEŠ / mesh = plural marker

[PLM] Jaritz #889 depicts a 'short vertical line abutting a longer horizontal line at its midpoint'. It means 'speak, call, tongue, middle, converse'. Graphic convention designed to bring out the idea of 'middle', the position associated in early thinking with the placement of the tongue in the mouth. Somewhat surprisingly, this simple element has been identified for PIE as *me, 'in the middle, into the middle'. *me is not regarded as meaning 'tongue'; that meaning

has been taken by a derivation from it, eme (for *îmî) [12174] another reading of the same sign, which represents 'teeth-middle' = 'tongue'. This compound can be found in PIE with *empi-, 'mosquito', an animal that definitely deserves to be named for its tongue.

uQQ me₃ [243x]= battle, combat cf. 12228 copula

12229 MES, meš₃ [56x] black [Gilgamesh was black! nextdoor on list to 1222A MI / gig2 main black]; [29x] = hero; manly; young man cf. Enki and the world order c113.221, Ninurta's exploits c162.310, Samsu-iluna & Inanna c2831.15 [NB computerized transl no ordinary 'tree' more like 'hero']) |
ĝešmes (ĝešmes, ĝešmeš₃) [81x] = tree| kišib (-la₂) [36x] = cylinder seal, sealed tablet; kišib-rah₂ .. with aux. = to seal

cf. 1231D [less vertical ge than 12229] UM reed (stylus?) stem + 4 var;

1207E DUB tablet | kišib₃ [17468x] = cylinder seal, sealed tablet

..

cpd BIL.GA.MEŠ (Sumerian: Bilgamesh; Akkad.: Gilgamesh) black hero of oldest written epic (quest for immortality) [1224B BIL₂ burnt + 120B5 GA young (bull) + 12229 mes (meš₃) black hero (next on the sign list is the more common black sign 1222A MI) ; and 1207E dub able to write = power connotation)]

..

1222A MI [<=cun-sign | Sumerian=>] ge₆, giggi (ge₆), gi₆, ĝi₆, gig₂ [941x] = to be black, night | ge/gi same as 12100 reed stylus => writing => knowledge => power = black | upper / high (class) cf. mi-iq-tum (miqtum, mi-ĝal₂-tum) = social class

**Inana's black
braided hair
7400CT**

1222A = MI / gig₂ = black

cf. dome of night sky - cpd ul₄-he₂ firmament, vault of sky
[12109 terror + 120F6 boundless]

..

Sumerians called themselves black people ⟨cuneiform⟩ ùĝ₃-
saĝ-gíg₂-ga [12326 ùĝ₃ people (KALAM Sumer) + 12295 saĝ head + 1222A gíg₂
black + 120B5 ga carry / aux.] see tablet examples; not just black plebs either, the

'First professors are BLACK!' ⟨cuneiform⟩ um-mi-a = scholar, expert,
craftsman [scholar 1231D UM reed stem (stylus/writing symbol, 1207E tablet var)
+ 1222A MI black + 12000 progeny]

ummia [EXPERT] (142x: ED IIIb, Old Akkadian, Ur III

expert, master craftsman

⟨cuneiform⟩ um-mi-a

Not just the Sumerians calling themselves black, the first professors are BLACK!

7000CT/5000ya	7500CT/4500ya	8000CT/4000ya	
14	110	18	PSD

..

diĝir [DEITY] (1837x: ED IIIb, Old Akkadian, Lagash II, Ur III
"deity, god, goddess"   **The gods are black too!**

[1]	⟨cuneiform⟩	diĝir (dingir)
[2]	⟨cuneiform⟩	dim₃-me-er (ES)
[3]	⟨cuneiform⟩	dim₃-me₈-er (ES)
[4]	⟨cuneiform⟩	dim₃-mi-ir (ES)
[5]	⟨cuneiform⟩	di-me₂-er (ES) PSD

And even Gilgamesh is black, see previous entry 12229

..

SUMERIAN

earth	lord	black
⟨cuneiform⟩	⟨cuneiform⟩	⟨cuneiform⟩
ki	en	gi
(kih	en	gih)
121A0	12097	1222A

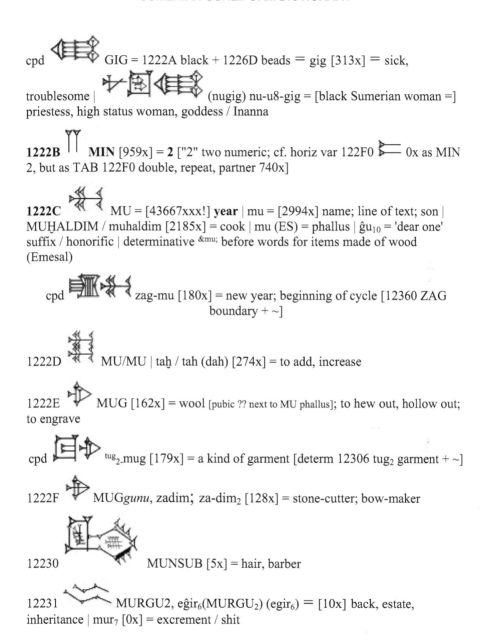

cpd GIG = 1222A black + 1226D beads = gig [313x] = sick,

troublesome | (nugig) nu-u8-gig = [black Sumerian woman =] priestess, high status woman, goddess / Inanna

1222B **MIN** [959x] = **2** ["2" two numeric; cf. horiz var 122F0 0x as MIN 2, but as TAB 122F0 double, repeat, partner 740x]

1222C MU = [43667xxx!] **year** | mu = [2994x] name; line of text; son | MUḪALDIM / muhaldim [2185x] = cook | mu (ES) = phallus | ĝu₁₀ = 'dear one' suffix / honorific | determinative μ before words for items made of wood (Emesal)

cpd zag-mu [180x] = new year; beginning of cycle [12360 ZAG boundary + ~]

1222D MU/MU | taḫ / tah (dah) [274x] = to add, increase

1222E MUG [162x] = wool [pubic ?? next to MU phallus]; to hew out, hollow out; to engrave

cpd ᵗᵘᵍ₂.mug [179x] = a kind of garment [determ 12306 tug₂ garment + ~]

1222F MUGgunu, zadim; za-dim₂ [128x] = stone-cutter; bow-maker

12230 MUNSUB [5x] = hair, barber

12231 MURGU2, eĝir₆(MURGU₂) (egir₆) = [10x] back, estate, inheritance | mur₇ [0x] = excrement / shit

12232 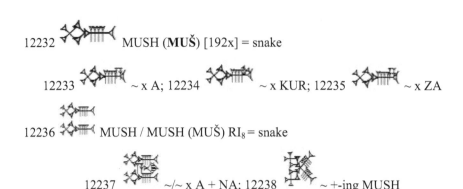 MUSH (**MUŠ**) [192x] = snake

12233 ~ x A; 12234 ~ x KUR; 12235 ~ x ZA

12236 MUSH / MUSH (**MUŠ**) RI_8 = snake

12237 ~/~ x A + NA; 12238 ~ +-ing MUSH

12239 $MUSH_3$ / $MUŠ_3$ = [107x] face, appearance; [81x] flat space, holy

area; [3x] curdle | sed_6 ($šed_{12}$) [11x #3 behind sed_4] = cold; winter .. cpd
sed_4 ($še_{17}$, $šed_{10}$) [34x; ~ + 12072 well-being] | $MUŠ_3INANNA$, INNIN = goddess |

1202D AN+ $MUŠ_3$ = ^{d}Inanna / Inanna

1223A $MUSH_3$ / $MUŠ_3$ x A | se_{24}, sed_3, $še_{12}$, $šed_9$ = winter, hibernate, rest, be
content

1223B ~ x A + DI; 1223C ~ x DI; 1223D ~*gunu*

1223E NA, niĝna = [114x] incense (burner); man; [32x] stone; pestle,
pounder

cpd ma-na / mina [9459x] = unit of weight; 1 mina = 60 shekels, 1
talent = 60 mina [3600 shekels]

1223F NA_2, NU_2 [419x] = to lie down (of people); to lay down; to be ill;

bed | NUD | cf. 12029 icon

cpd $ba-na_2$ = 12040 BA split, open + ~

12240　　NAGA, naĝa [2521x] = potash (potassium compound often used in agriculture); soap | NAG₂, NISABA₂ = tornado

cpd　　DINGIR.NAGA.ZAG.SAL, ᵈnisaba za₃-mi₂ = Nisaba praised [1202D AN god + 12240 NAGA + 12360 za₃ + 122A9 mi₂ cuneus]

12241　~ INVERTED; 12242　~ x SHU tenu; 12243

~ opp ~

12244　　NAGAR [666x] = carpenter

12245　　NAM, nutillu | buru₅ = [4x] locust

12246　　NAM = [567x] determined order; will, testament; fate, destiny | bir₅ [35x incl 12 ED IIIa] = locust | sin₂ = district | sim = [var < 16x] smell, sniff, filter, swallow | nam-tar = destiny | nam-ra = booty, spoils, captive

cpd　　nam-mah = NAMMAH, earliest known mathematician, see 122B9 [~ + 12224 mah great]

12247　　NAM₂ = prefix lord / official; thought, planning ??

12248 ![NE sign] NE, (bí / bi₂) | de₃ [25x] bring / carry (collect) | šeĝ₆ (še₆, šeg₆) [261x] = to cook; to dry a field | izi = [257x] fire (pottery), brazier | kum₂ [78x] = hot | bi₂ in compounds | nen, ne, ne-en, ne-e [101x] = this, these | bil [7x] = burn

 Jaritz #339 burning torch

cpds

![NE-A sign] NE-A = refine [~ + 12000 A water]

![il-i-de sign] il₂-i-de₃ = collect firewood [1214D il₂ carry + 1213F I "5" + 12248 de₃ collect]

![NE-SU-UB sign] NE-SU-UB = to be on fire, kissing [~ + 122E2 SU submerge, flesh + 12312 UB praise, ruin]

12249 ![NE x A sign] NE x A | eš₁₃ [0x] = cold | cf. 12239 sed₄ cold; winter

1224A ![NE x UD sign] NE x UD

1224B ![NE sheshig sign] NE sheshig / šešig, BIL₂ | gibil [671x] = new, renew; firewood | bil₂ [43x] = burn / burnt

cpd ![BIL.GA.MEŠ sign] BIL.GA.MEŠ (Sumerian: Bilgamesh [cf. Billjim!]; Akkad.: Gilgamesh) black hero of oldest written epic [1224B BIL₂ burnt + 120B5 GA young (bull) + 12229 mes (meš) black hero]

1224C ![NI sign] NI <= cun-sign | Sumerian => Ì / i₃, IÀ / ia₃, I, lí / li₂ | (syll.: bè, lé, lí, né) i₃ = [8654x] oil; butter; container for oil vegetable oil, fat | ZAL [2798x] = to pass time; to get up early; to finish, come to an end (come to pass); to dissolve, melt, disintegrate, break down, collapse; to quake; sensual aura / connotation | cpd

![na sign] na₄ [527x] = stone; stone weight | determinative &na4; stones | cf. 12155

![IR sign] IR ask; perfume

1224D  NI x E

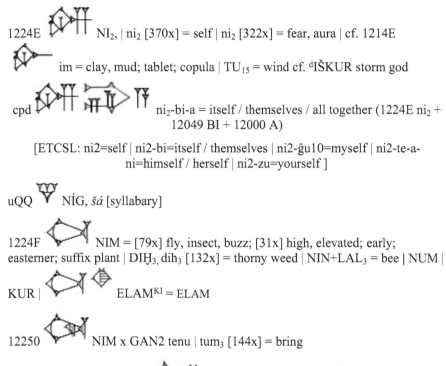

1224E NI$_2$, | ni$_2$ [370x] = self | ni$_2$ [322x] = fear, aura | cf. 1214E

im = clay, mud; tablet; copula | TU$_{15}$ = wind cf. ^{d}IŠKUR storm god

cpd ni$_2$-bi-a = itself / themselves / all together (1224E ni$_2$ +
12049 BI + 12000 A)

[ETCSL: ni2=self | ni2-bi=itself / themselves | ni2-ĝu10=myself | ni2-te-a-
ni=himself / herself | ni2-zu=yourself]

uQQ NÍG, *šá* [syllabary]

1224F NIM = [79x] fly, insect, buzz; [31x] high, elevated; early;
easterner; suffix plant | DIH$_3$, dih$_3$ [132x] = thorny weed | NIN+LAL$_3$ = bee | NUM |

KUR | ELAM^{KI} = ELAM

12250 NIM x GAN2 tenu | tum$_3$ [144x] = bring

12251 NIM x GAR + GAN2 tenu

12252 NINDA$_2$ = [39x] seed-funnel [cf. hand-scoop Jaritz #347 see
12258 below]; fish ??; breeding bull | INDA = [0x!] bread, food | cf. much more

common 120FB NINDA [11296x]

NINDA$_2$ Variants

12253 ~ x AN, ŠAM$_3$ = buy, price ; 12254 ~ x ASH; 12255
~ x ASH + ASH;

12256 ~ x GUD ; 12257 ~ x ME + GAN2 tenu

12258 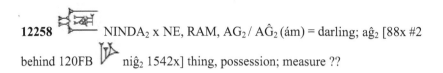 NINDA₂ x NE, RAM, AG₂ / AĜ₂ (ám) = darling; aĝ₂ [88x #2

behind 120FB niĝ₂ 1542x] thing, possession; measure ??

Jaritz #362 a combination sign which, rather incongruously, depicts a "hand-scoop' (#347) enclosing #339 [12248 NE] burning torch, signifying the 'heat of passionate love' [encapsulated fire].

cpd ki-aĝ₂ (ki-ag₂) [666x] = **to love** [121A0 KI cosmic world + 12258 ag₂ heat of passionate love]

12259 ~ x NUN

1225A NINDA₂ x SHE / ŠE, ŠAM₂ (NINDA₂ x ŠE + A AN variants) = price

1225B ~ x SHE + A AN; 1225C ~ x SHE + ASH; 1225D ~ x SHE + ASH + ASH;

1225E ~ x U2 + ASH; 1225F ~ x USH

..

12260 NISAG, MURU₂, MURUB₄ [44x] = middle; cuneus | cf. uQQ

murub₆ (muru₁₃); murub₂; rump, rump; knob; mouth; gate (of city or large building); space between, distance; link; hips | ITI *gunû*

12261 NU [785x] = **not** (negation: "no", negative); without, un-; genitals; sperm; offspring | NU-GAL₂ = nonexistent | NU-TIL = incomplete | *True Etym.* nu => no

12262 NU₁₁ | ĝešnu (gešnu) [3x] = light | duri [0x] = male; to be virile

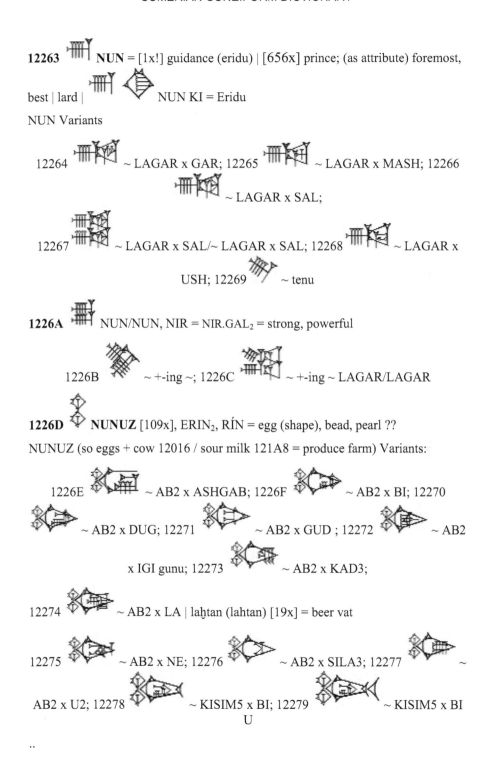

12263 NUN = [1x!] guidance (eridu) | [656x] prince; (as attribute) foremost,

best | lard | NUN KI = Eridu

NUN Variants

12264 ~ LAGAR x GAR; 12265 ~ LAGAR x MASH; 12266 ~ LAGAR x SAL;

12267 ~ LAGAR x SAL/~ LAGAR x SAL; 12268 ~ LAGAR x

USH; 12269 ~ tenu

1226A NUN/NUN, NIR = NIR.GAL$_2$ = strong, powerful

1226B ~ +-ing ~; 1226C ~ +-ing ~ LAGAR/LAGAR

1226D NUNUZ [109x], ERIN$_2$, RÍN = egg (shape), bead, pearl ??

NUNUZ (so eggs + cow 12016 / sour milk 121A8 = produce farm) Variants:

1226E ~ AB2 x ASHGAB; 1226F ~ AB2 x BI; 12270 ~ AB2 x DUG; 12271 ~ AB2 x GUD ; 12272 ~ AB2 x IGI gunu; 12273 ~ AB2 x KAD3;

12274 ~ AB2 x LA | laḫtan (lahtan) [19x] = beer vat

12275 ~ AB2 x NE; 12276 ~ AB2 x SILA3; 12277 ~ AB2 x U2; 12278 ~ KISIM5 x BI; 12279 ~ KISIM5 x BI
U

..

1227A PA | ugula = **[9794x]** foreman, overseer | bá [293x] = wing; branch, frond | gidru / ĝidri = [129x] sceptre | sìg = to beat | garza = office | SIG hit e.g. cpd SIG-UZU ~ TUD beat whip

1227B PAD, ŠUK /SHUK, šukur$_2$ /shukur$_2$ (šuk, šuku) = [1335x] food allocation, ration | [56x] to break (into bits); pierce

1227C PAN, tir$_5$ [63x] = bow; geometric figure {PSD} | cf bow-maker, PANA = bow, arrow

1227D PAP, KUR$_2$ [607x] = unit of capacity based on a vessel size; PAP = [86x] relation; first and foremost, pre-eminent; father; male, virile; brother | PAB =

protect | PA$_5$ = canal | cpd DIM [13x] = to check; to approach

1227E PESH2 / PEŠ$_2$, PIŠ$_2$ [55x] = mouse

1227F **PI** (bì) [269x] tal$_2$, | geshtu / geštu, geshtug / geštug = **ear**, hear, reason, intelligence, wisdom, understanding

PI Variants:

12280 ~ x A; 12281 ~ x AB; 12282 ~ x BI; 12283 ~ x BU;

12284 ~ x E; 12285 ~ x I; 12286 ~ x IB; 12287 ~ x U;

12288 ~ x U2; 12289 ~ +-ing PI

..

1228A PIRIG (PIRIĜ) [198x] = lion

1228B PIRIG (PIRIĜ) x KAL, NIB = leopard

1228C PIRIG (PIRIĜ) x UD, UG = tiger

1228D   PIRIG (PIRIĜ) x ZA, AZ, AS = bear

1228E   PIRIG (PIRIĜ) *opp* PIRIG

1228F RA, rah₂ [597x] = to beat, kill; to break, crush; to flood; to thresh (grain with a flail) | aux. ~ -ra | see also notes on evolution [PLM (Patrick Ryan '2008)]: – wheel rim with four spokes over curled horn suggests 'back' over 'tall'; also 'stir'; emphasizes flood

cpd im-ta-e₃-a-ra = sunrise [1214E IM mood + 122EB TA much + cpd UD-DU sunrise + 12000 A bemoan + 1228F RA beat thresh]

12290 RAB, raba [37x] = clamp; neck stock; hoop ??

12291 RI = [475x] to lay down, cast, place; to set in place, imbue; to lean on; to impose; to throw down; to release, let go; to walk along; to pour out, impregnate; to lead away | re [130x] = "that" | auxiliary verb, sar-ri / sar-re 122AC | distant | cf. 12137

12292 RU, shub / šub [495x] = fall, defeat; throw (boomerang) | ru [92x; #2 behind 12291 RI (above)] imbue; impose; release, pour out; impregnate

12293 ▥ SA = braided, string, net, sinew, muscle | determinative &sa; before braided items

12294 ⌖ SAG, sağ, nutillu = head [rare, always 12295]

SAĜ Variants:

12295 ⌖ SAG, **SAĜ** (pron. sang), SUR$_{14}$ [3582x]= head; person / people; capital

cpd ⌖ sağ-ğa$_2$ = head basket [12295 sağ head + 120B7 ğa2 basket]

12296 ⌖ ~ x A; 12297 ⌖ ~ x DU; 12298 ⌖ ~ x DUB; 12299

⌖ ~ x HA; 1229A ⌖ ~ x KAK; 1229B ⌖ ~ x KUR; 1229C

⌖ ~ x LUM; 1229D ⌖ ~ x MI; 1229E ⌖ ~ x NUN; 1229F

⌖ ~ x SAL; **122A0** ⌖ ~ x SHID; 122A1 ⌖ ~ x TAB; 122A2

⌖ ~ x U2; 122A3 ⌖ ~ x UB; 122A4 ⌖ ~ x UM; 122A5

⌖ ~ x UR; 122A6 ⌖ ~ x USH; 122A7 ⌖ ~/~; 122A8 ⌖

~ *gunu*

..

122A9 ⟁ SAL, mug, gal₄ (gala), murub (muru₁₃), munus [3079x] = cuneus ⩣
apotheosis of woman, goddess, matriarch, queen | mi₂ = [13x - all ED IIIb] praise;
CVNE | determinative before female names &f;
[The scribes who invented writing 5000 years ago clearly had no inhibitions about
the basis for the design of their cuneiform, nor should we bowdlerize [etym.:
Thomas Bowdler expurgated William Shakespeare (aka Edward de Vere) '1822] for
hypocritical luddites / puritans who are still happy to plagiarize the technology
revolution started by the Sumerians, and it may well have been the inspiration for
the whole style ~ cunei.form = cuneus writing.

Scratching and dragging a pointed stylus would not have been near as effective and
enduring for us to be able to read now. And it can be no coincidence that the
Sumerian apotheosis of 'woman' through the cuneus-shaped **v** sign has come down
to us as the first letter of vagina, a fundamental example of *True Etymology*.]

Enheduanna – earliest known author and poet was female
And not only were the first scholars black, the earliest known author and poet was

female (and most likely black), Enheduanna ⟨cuneiform⟩ 7715-
7750CT (2285-2250 plag) ... Westenholz edited a fragmentary hymn dedicated to
Enheduanna indicating her apotheosis... [Wik]; she was totally lost to history until
her tablets were unearthed in '1926 [Nisaba] by Leonard Woolley [born '1880 in 13
Southwold Road just around the corner from King's Place (now BSix College
Brooke House - East London Hackney-Stratford where the '2012 Olympics Games
were held) where Edward de Vere wrote 'Shake-speares Sonnets' - only because he
was setup by another forgotten proto-feminist, 2nd wife Elizabeth Trentham]; she
represented a strong and creative personality, an educated woman, and one who
fulfilled diverse roles in a complex society, not unlike women's aspirations
today...[Jane Roberts]; "My goddess gave birth to your god" ... Assyriologist
William Hallo referred to her as "The Sumerian Shakespeare". But given that she
preceded Shakespeare by several thousand years, it might be more apt to dub the
bard "The English Enheduanna" [Kristin Agudelo's notablewomen]; or
"Enheduanna of Tudor Literature" [chickhistory]; ironically also lost to history is
Susan de Vere, Shakespeare's Daughter and Producer of the First Folio.

"My king, something has been created that no one has created before."

The earliest known author and poet was female

ENHEDUANNA
7715-7750CT
(2285-2250 plag)

cpds:

emi (e$_2$-mi$_2$) [219x] = queen's household [1208D e$_2$ house + 122A9 mi$_2$ cuneus]

NIN = lady, mistress [122A9 cuneus + 12306 garment]; e$_5$ = princely ?? | e$_5$, ereš

nin$_9$ [247x] = sister [~ + 121AA ku rump]

mussa (mi$_2$-us$_2$-sa$_2$) [53x] = son / daughter in-law [122A9 mi$_2$ cuneus; praise + 12351 us$_2$ phallus + 12072 sa$_2$ law]

geme$_2$ [4025x] = slave woman [~ + 121B3 mountains - Sumerians associated mountains with breasts and caves with cuneus... mythicjourneys.org]

MURUB$_2$ = cuneus, rump [~ + 121EC priestess] cf. uQQ murub$_6$ (muru$_{13}$), 12260 murub$_4$ (muru$_2$)

gal$_4$-la-na = cuneus – bending over, show [122A9 gal$_4$ cuneus + 121B7 LA bending over / rump, show + 1223E NA man, pestle, pounder]

True Etym.: gala (festive dress, make merry) cf. also GALA-TUR young male performer [12351 us$_2$ phallus + 121AA KU rump + 12309 TUR young]

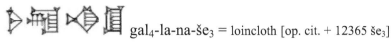 gal₄-la-na-še₃ = loincloth [op. cit. + 12365 še₃]

gal₄-la-ĝa₂ = cuneus (deeper sense) [122A9 gal₄ cuneus + 121B7
LA bending over / rump + 120B7 ĝa₂ house;

ETCSL: A balbale [12044] Dumuzi-Inanna "Plough my... (c40816.B.31) the moist
and well-watered ground (c40816.B.27)"]

Inana's "loincloth of
7 divine powers" (Ur)

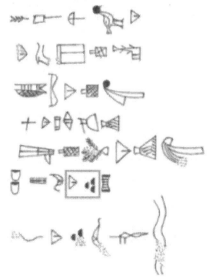

Proto Cuneiform – see Ref.

122AA SAL LAGAB x ASH2

122AB  SANGA$_2$ / saĝa$_2$ = [12x] priest

122AC SAR [377x] = to **write** || sar [4917x] = garden; a unit of area; a unit of volume | SAKAR, MU$_2$, kiri$_6$ = (fruit) plantation, orchard | determinative $^{&sar;}$ after garden / vegetables | šar [26x #2 behind 122B9 šar$_2$] = 3600; totality, world; numerous

[PLM] Jaritz #281 archaic variant of SAR - knot in a cord, fasten together - write - line up characters in a fixed order

cpd 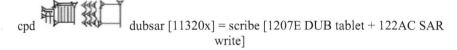 dubsar [11320x] = scribe [1207E DUB tablet + 122AC SAR write]

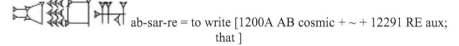 ab-sar-re = to write [1200A AB cosmic + ~ + 12291 RE aux; that]

cpd sar-ra-ka-ni = garden plot [122AC SAR garden + 1228F RA thresh + 12157 KA mouth + 1224C NI digest]

122AD SHA / ša = [74x] heart (variant cf. 122AE); [3x] official

uQQ šá=NÍG [syllabary; numeric??]

122AE SHA$_3$ / **ŠA$_3$**, šag$_4$, tibula = [10808x] **heart**, center, interior

cpd a-sag4 [9387x] = field, surface math.

ŠA$_3$ Variants:

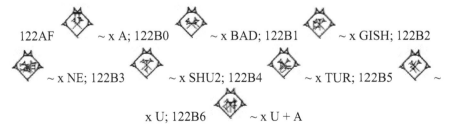

122AF ~ x A; 122B0 ~ x BAD; 122B1 ~ x GISH; 122B2

~ x NE; 122B3 ~ x SHU2; 122B4 ~ x TUR; 122B5 ~

x U; 122B6 ~ x U + A

..

122B7   SHA$_6$, SAG$_9$ [826x] = good, sweet, beautiful

122B8   SHAB$_6$ (šab$_6$) qqq [cf. 1219A KAM$_2$; numeric??]

122B9 ● SHAR$_2$ / šar$_2$ [245x] = 3600; totality, world; numerous [*True Etym.*: 360° circle, inventors sexagesimal system; math table; etc.] [šar$_2$ *is formed by making a circular indentation with the end of the stylus*]

šar [3600] 245x: ED IIIa, Ur III   [PSD]
totality, world;   Oldest Math Table=→   made by Nammah
numerous; 3600   (Shuruppag) 7500CT
● šar$_2$ 1st 2 cols: identical lengths descending 600 to 60 rods (3600 to 360m)
▒☐ šar   col3: square area of their product;   History Math Tables - from Sumer to Speadsheets
●● šar$_2$-šar$_2$ using 12072 ⬦ = SA equals ⬦   Martin C Kelly
invention of sexigesimal/360°circle

	7000CT/3000*pl*	7500CT / 2500*pl*	8000CT / 2000*pl*
[1]	3	1	181
[2]		25	1
[3]		3	22

122BA   SHE / ŠE | niga, nigu = [28315x!] barley, grain; unit of length / area / volume / weight; shekel | True Etymology: origin of Hebrew term for money 'shekel' re price of bushel of grain | niga [12565x] = to be fattened

Money, like certain other essential elements in civilization, is an institution that goes way further back than we are taught to believe ... the oldest coin currency that we know is a Sumerian bronze piece dating from before 7000CT / 3000plagio.

'On one side of the coin is a representation of a sheaf of wheat, and on the other, Ishtar, the goddess of fertility.
The Sumerians called it the "Shekel" where "She" meant wheat, "Kel" [12086] was a measurement similar to a bushel, hence this coin was a symbol of a value of one bushel of wheat. (The word "shekel" survives in modern Hebrew as Israel's monetary unit.) The original shekel had as its purpose payment for sacred prostitution at the temple of Ishtar, which was the temple of life and death. The temple, as well as being a ritual center, was the storage place for the reserves of wheat that supported the priesthood, and also the community in lean times. So farmers fulfilled their religious and social obligations by bringing their contributions of wheat to the temple, and receiving in exchange a shekel coin, entitling them to a visit with the temple prostitutes at the festival time. All this also must be understood in its cultural context: The sacred prostitutes were representatives of the goddess, and relations with them was relations with the goddess of fertility herself, nothing to take lightly...' The Future of Money, Bernard Lietaer '1997

..
'...coinage was arranged according to the sexagesimal numbering system developed earlier by the Sumerians
ie. 1, 60 [1x60], and 3600 [122B9 (60x60)]
...lowest denomination was a "shekel", then a "mina" [1223E] and finally a "talent" [12118]
1 mina = 60 shekels. 1 talent = 60 mina [3600 shekels]. The mina weighted about 500 gms., and the talent about 30 kgs.
These coins were used to pay for property, buy goods and services, pay fines, pay taxes, etc.
Some examples of the use of the shekel from one of the later law codes inscribed on the cuneiform tablets:
"The price of one gur [12125] of barley is one shekel of silver'.
 "The price of 2 gurs of salt is one shekel of silver".
"The price of one hal [1212C] seed is one shekel of silver".

89

SUMERIAN CUNEIFORM DICTIONARY

"The wage of a labourer is one shekel of silver and his food one ban of barley and he has to serve for this wage for one month"...
Some information on the relative value of the coins and the wealth that each represented... The scribe is lauding the benevolent king for his protection of the poor. "He saw to it that ... the man of one shekel did not fall a prey to the man of one mina (sixty shekels) ..."'
[more: moriancumr2.blogspot.com.au/2012/04/sumerian-money.html]
..

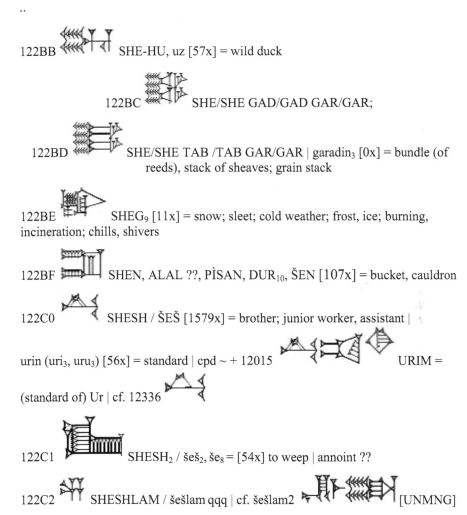

122BB   SHE-HU, uz [57x] = wild duck

122BC   SHE/SHE GAD/GAD GAR/GAR;

122BD   SHE/SHE TAB /TAB GAR/GAR | garadin$_3$ [0x] = bundle (of reeds), stack of sheaves; grain stack

122BE   SHEG$_9$ [11x] = snow; sleet; cold weather; frost, ice; burning, incineration; chills, shivers

122BF   SHEN, ALAL ??, PÌSAN, DUR$_{10}$, ŠEN [107x] = bucket, cauldron

122C0   SHESH / ŠEŠ [1579x] = brother; junior worker, assistant |

urin (uri$_3$, uru$_3$) [56x] = standard | cpd ~ + 12015   URIM =

(standard of) Ur | cf. 12336

122C1   SHESH$_2$ / šeš$_2$, še$_8$ = [54x] to weep | annoint ??

122C2   SHESHLAM / šešlam qqq | cf. šešlam2   [UNMNG]

122C3 ![cuneiform] SHID / ŠID, ŠIT / SHIT! ŠITI, LAG | saĝĝa [1862x] (sanga, sangu, saĝa₈) = an official, the chief administrator of a temple household | nesaĝ₂ (nesag₂) [661x] = first-fruit offering; a storage place | šid [292x] = count(ing); number; half (shares); to count [calculate] | silaĝ [0x] = body part

122C4 ![cuneiform] ~ x A; 122C5 ![cuneiform] ~ x IM

122C6 ![cuneiform] SHIM / šim [819x] = beer, beer malt - cf. 12049 ![cuneiform] kaš [13889x] | [35x] type of basin | ŠEM, LUNGA = scent (aromatic substance)

ŠIM Variants

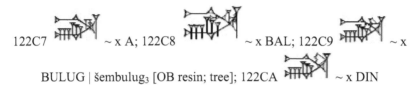

122C7 ![cuneiform] ~ x A; 122C8 ![cuneiform] ~ x BAL; 122C9 ![cuneiform] ~ x

BULUG | šembulug₃ [OB resin; tree]; 122CA ![cuneiform] ~ x DIN

122CB ![cuneiform] ~ x GAR, bappir [64x #3 behind 1204B ![cuneiform] bappir₃] = an ingredient in beer-making, spice

122CC ![cuneiform] ~ x IGI;

122CD ![cuneiform] ~ x IGI *gunu* | šembi [38x] = eye makeup, kohl; antimony paste; to anoint, smear on

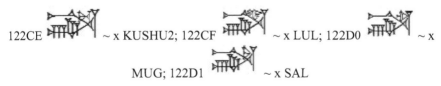

122CE ![cuneiform] ~ x KUSHU2; 122CF ![cuneiform] ~ x LUL; 122D0 ![cuneiform] ~ x

MUG; 122D1 ![cuneiform] ~ x SAL

..

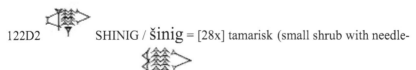

122D2 ![cuneiform] SHINIG / **šinig** = [28x] tamarisk (small shrub with needle-

shaped leaves) | cf 12240

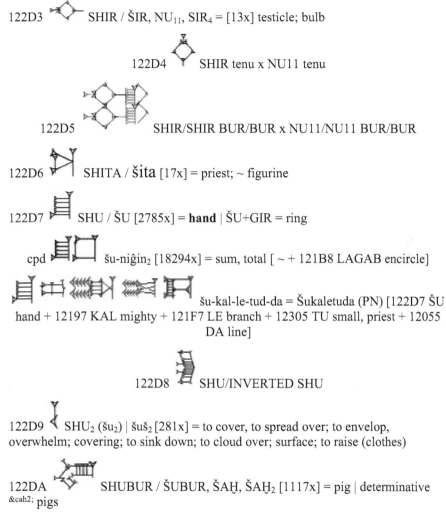

122D3 SHIR / ŠIR, NU₁₁, SIR₄ = [13x] testicle; bulb

122D4 SHIR tenu x NU11 tenu

122D5 SHIR/SHIR BUR/BUR x NU11/NU11 BUR/BUR

122D6 SHITA / šita [17x] = priest; ~ figurine

122D7 SHU / ŠU [2785x] = **hand** | ŠU+GIR = ring

cpd šu-niĝin₂ [18294x] = sum, total [~ + 121B8 LAGAB encircle]

šu-kal-le-tud-da = Šukaletuda (PN) [122D7 ŠU hand + 12197 KAL mighty + 121F7 LE branch + 12305 TU small, priest + 12055 DA line]

122D8 SHU/INVERTED SHU

122D9 SHU₂ (šu₂) | šuš₂ [281x] = to cover, to spread over; to envelop, overwhelm; covering; to sink down; to cloud over; surface; to raise (clothes)

122DA SHUBUR / ŠUBUR, ŠAH, ŠAH₂ [1117x] = pig | determinative
&cah2; pigs

cf uQQ šul [shul; 305x] = manly; youth; young man

122DB SI = [401x] to fill, load up; to draw water; to brew beer | [262x] horn | finger; fret

cpd bi₂-ib-si-si = fill [12248 bi₂ carry + 12141 IB oval + 122DB SI fill]

si-si-de₃ = fill and carry

im-mi-ib₂-si-si = draw / fill (water from well) [1214E IM storm, anger + 1222A MI black + 12308 ib2 cross-beam (of well) + 122DB SI x2 fill]

u₅ = high water [12137 mušen bird + ~]

[PLM] a combination, the top element... 'sitting bird', 'egg-like' = 'bird' (but also possibly 'brood')

122DC   SI *gunu*

122DD   SIG [343x] = weak; low; thin; narrow

122DE   SIG₄, šeg₁₂ [572x] = clay / mud brick | MURGU [363x] = shoulder, back

[PLM] sig(a)₄, '(dried) brick', depicts 'three bricks/tiles forming a zig-zag pattern':

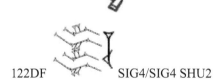

122DF   SIG4/SIG4 SHU2

122E0   SIK₂, SIG₂, SIKI [4753x] = wool, fleece; hair; (animal's) pelt [*cf. True Etym. siki => silk*]

122E1   SILA₃ **[43696x!!!]** = a unit of capacity (= 1 litre, Oxford Handbook Cuneiform p64); a vessel

122E2   SU, KUŠ [3818x] = skin, hide, leather, fur; person; [54x] submerge, skin games; [495x] flesh, body, to be inside, entrails | determinative &kuc; before words for items made of leather

122E3   SU/SU

uQQ ![glyph] SU₄, SI₄ [184x] = to be red, brown

122E4 ![glyph] SUD, ŠUD / shud [488x] = distant; remote, long-lasting; profound | SIR, BU *gunû* = pull; spread; sail; run

122E5 ![glyph] SUD₂ = grind, bite ??

122E6 ![glyph] SUHUR [3x] = to trim or comb the hair | head hair | cf. munsub₂

122E7 ![glyph] SUM, ŠUM₂, SI₃ = give [*True Etymology:* 'sum' (total, add up); Greek 'sigma'] | sig₁₀ (si) [836x] = to cast; to fashion

cpd ![glyph] im-ma-ni-sig₁₀ = to cast (an eye) [1214E IM mud, storm + 12220 MA approach + 1224C NI finish + 122E7 cast]

122E8 ![glyph] SUMASH / sumaš | sumaš^ku6 [49x] = an oceanic fish

122E9 ![glyph] SUR [82x] = to squeeze, press; to flash; to drip; to rain; to milk - cpd

![glyph] ![glyph] ĝeš3+sur = phallus + squeeze / milk = piss, urinate, masturbate |

[82x] = half | cf. 120FB ![glyph] bread; thing

122EA ![glyph] SUR₉ = [plectrum, musical??]

122EB ![glyph] TA (dá) [85x] = what? | as much as (math./ quantity), from [preposition]

122EC ![glyph] TA = asterisk [= star = TAra] cf. 1202D

122ED ![glyph] TA x HI, LAL₃ [241x]= syrup, honey

122EE ![glyph] TA x MI; 122EF ![glyph] TA gunu

122F0 ⊨ **TAB, MIN** [0x!] = **2** ["2" / two numeric] | TAB [740x] = to double; to repeat; companion, partner, friend | cf. more used 1222B 𝕀𝕀 [959x] | *True Etym.:* tab (key); tabulate

122F1 TAB/TAB NI/NI DISH/DISH

122F2 TAB sq

122F3 **TAG** [266x] = to touch, take hold of; to bind – *True Etym.:* tag, touch (tuku); to attack | šum [63x] = slaughter | TUKU₅ [151x] = beat, strike of cloth; to weave | TIBIR [26x] = hand | ZIL₂ = good, beneficent

122F4 ~ x BI;**122F5** ~ x GUD;**122F6** ~ x SHE;**122F7** ~ x SHU;

122F8 ~ x TUG2;**122F9** ~ x UD

122FA **TAK₄**, (da₁₃) [667x] = to set aside, leave behind; to save, keep back, *hold back*

122FB **TAR** = [237x] to cut down; to untie, loosen; to scatter, disperse | sila [238x] = street | kud, ku₅ [1111x] = to break off, deduct; to separate, cut off; to cut; to incise; to decide; to make clear | disease

122FC TE = cheek; to pierce, penetrate, [31x] membrane | cpd

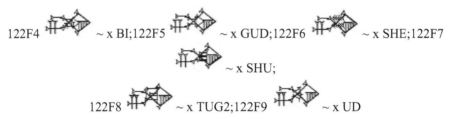

im-ma-te = approach, landing [1214E IM wind + 12220 flow + 122FC TE approach, land cf. 12312 UB as in kiss, suck]

cpd (im/) ni₂-te-a-ni = penetrate; inspect [inspected 1214E IM storm + 122FC TE cheek; penetrate; membrane + 12000 A cry of woe + 1224C NI quiver]

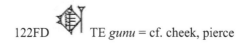

122FD TE *gunu* = cf. cheek, pierce

122FE ⟨sign⟩ TI, TIL₃ [770x] = life, to live; to sit (down); to dwell | ᵁᶻᵁTI = RIB

122FF ⟨sign⟩ TI tenu

12300 ⟨sign⟩ TIL [627x] = complete(d); old, long-lasting; to end | ÚŠ, EŠE₃~AŠ.U | SUMUN = sun, old | cf. ⟨sign⟩ BAD 12041

12301 ⟨sign⟩ TIR [404x] = forest, wood; mud

12302 ⟨sign⟩ ~ x TAK4 ; 12303 ⟨sign⟩ ~/~; 12304 ⟨sign⟩ ~/~
GAD/GAD GAR/GAR

12305 ⟨sign⟩ TU = priest [1x!] | sheep [4x!] | [16x] small | TU+TURᴹᵁŠᴱᴺ = little dove

12306 ⟨sign⟩ TUG, TUG₂ [5078x] = textile, garment (TU₉, dul₅; [379x] bar-dul₅) | usually as determinative ᵃⁿᵈ ᵗᵘᵍ²; garments | eš₂ | še₃, = towards | umuš (uš₄) [52x] = (fore)thought, plan(ning); understanding; instruction; consideration, sagacity | gi₇, gir₁₅, zi₃, zid₂ | azlag₂ = fuller (cleans thickens woven cloth) | TUG₂, TU₉, NAM₂ | cf.

12247 ⟨sign⟩ | *True Etym.*: Roman toga

cpd ⟨sign⟩ ᵗᵘᵍ²dara₄ = (Inanna's) loincloth, sash, G-String, belt [~ + 12071 dara4 = red, brown, blood]

12307 ⟨sign⟩ TUK, tuku = powerful able-bodied (cpd a₂-tuku); proud | TUG = anger

12308 ⟨sign⟩ TUM, (du₄) | ib₂ [36x] = hips; middle | ib₂ [35x] = angry; to curse | tum [19x] cross-beam| cf. mi-iq-tum (miqtum, mi-ĝal₂-tum) social class

12309 ⟨sign⟩ TUR | DUMU [28245xxx!] = child, son; apprentice | TUR [1719x] small; to reduce, diminish; to subtract; young

cpd ⟨sign⟩ dumu-munus [660x] = daughter [~ + 122A9 MUNUS cuneus]

⟨sign⟩ lu₂-tur [35x] = son [121FD lu₂ *hot rod* + ~]

1230A  TUR/TUR ZA/ZA

1230B ◁ **U** (vowel, basic cuneus); "**10**"; BUR₃ = hole | UḪ₇ = curse, bewitch |

121E5 ▨ NÍĜINxU) = PÚ = well (encircled area+hole) | šu₄ [24x] = totality, world | burud$_x$(U) (bur₃, buru₃) [49x] = breach, hole; depression, low-lying area, depth; to perforate / penetrate; deep | šu₄ = anus | šuš₂ (šu₄) [74x #2 behind 122D9 šu₂] = to cover, to spread over; to envelop, overwhelm; covering; to sink down; to cloud over; surface; to raise | bur₃ [54x #2 behind 12053 ▧ BUR 67x] = a unit of area; a unit of volume | ge₁₄ = stylus cuneus | [*winkelhaken* = angle hook]

[PLM] ○ means 'hole', and reads both u, '(oral) cavity', and hu3 'anus ('anal sphincter' or 'anal cavity')'. This is supported by another reading of this same sign: *šu4 (for *šü4), 'excrement-palm', the left hand being used mandatorily for the hygiene of unclean bodily functions. It is, to this day, a serious insult to offer a MidEasterner the left hand as a greeting because of the traditional use of the left hand.

1230C ⟨⟩ U-GUD, ul [161x] = distant time

cpd niĝul (nigul) ▧⟨⟩ niĝ₂-ul (nig₂-ul) [33x] = an everlasting possession [▧ = "Mugsar Benefactor whose family has been assigned a sign, cpd or section forever!"; asset; eternity, immortality; cf. etym. god | 120FB niĝ₂ possession + 1230C ul distant time]

1230D ⟪⟪ U+U+U | ESH / EŠ = 30 (numeric) | UŠU₃ | SIN = moon

1230E ▨ U/U PA/PA GAR/GAR

1230F ▧ U/U SUR/SUR | garadin₉ = sheaf, bundle (of reeds)

12310 ▧ U/U U rev/U rev

12311 ▥ U₂ [4129x] = plant(s); food; bread, loaf; grass; herb; pasture; firewood | determinative ˢᵘ²; plants

[12147] ù / u3 [6340x] = and; but; also

12312 UB = [78x] corner | ar$_2$ = [56x] praise, fame; [11x] ruin

12313 **UD** ud / u$_4$ **[29106xxx!]** = **sun, day,** time / "Once, ..."; summer, heat, fever | UTU | TAM, ZALAG, ZIMBIR (~UD.KIB.NUN) è (~UD.DU), ZABAR UD BABBAR |
BABBAR = white, shining | ZABAR = bronze | determinative $^{\&zabar;}$ bronze | ÀH = dried, withered

cpd e3 (UD-DU) [1850x] = to leave, to go out; to thread, hang on a string; to remove, take away; to bring out; to enter; to bring in; to raise (sunrise), rear (a child); to sow; to rave; to winnow; to measure (grain) roughly (with a stick); to rent [~ + 1207A DU]

 im-ta-e$_3$-a-ra = sunrise

 ud-ba = day (open, halved, noon?, Later?) [~ + 12040 BA]

UD Variants:

12314 UD KUSHU2 | *úḫ* [syl.] = weathervane??; 12315 UD x BAD ;

12316 UD x MI

12317 UD x U + U + U | ITI (UD×EŠ) itud, itid [2145x cf 36175x ??] = moon, month

12318 UD x U + U + U *gunu*

12319 UD *gunu* | murub$_6$ (muru$_{13}$) [446x] = cuneus, rump (rear view) – cf.

12260 murub$_4$

1231A  UD *sheshig (šešig),* itud$_x$, ITI | UD x EŠ ITI$_2$ ~ ITI x BAD = month [0x!]

1231B UD *sheshig* x BAD

1231C UDUG = a demon (of desert, mountain, sea, tomb); ~ figurine ??

1231D **UM** = [34x] reed (stylus? writing / black hero comes next to wheel UMBIN!), stem of

cf. 1207E DUB tablet; 12229 mes (meš$_3$), kišib black hero

It's not just the Sumerians calling themselves black, **the first professors are**

BLACK! 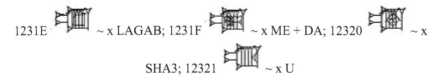 um-mi-a = scholar, expert, craftsman [scholar 1231D UM reed stem (stylus/writing symbol, 1207E tablet var) + 1222A MI black + 12000 progeny]

1231E ~ x LAGAB; 1231F ~ x ME + DA; 12320 ~ x

SHA3; 12321 ~ x U

Invention of the Wheel

12322   UMBIN = **wheel** | cf. **1232B**

UR₂ (lynchpin), 122FA   TAK₄, = hold back (the King's fancy hub caps)

umbin [WHEEL] (94x: ED IIIb. wr. umbin "wheel"   **PSD**

[1]   umbin   'Invention of the wheel'

7000CT/**3000**/pl	7500CT / **2500**pl	8000CT/**2000**pl
6	72	11

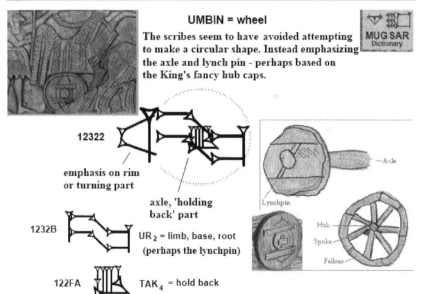

UMBIN = wheel

The scribes seem to have avoided attempting to make a circular shape. Instead emphasizing the axle and lynch pin - perhaps based on the King's fancy hub caps.

MUG SAR
Dictionary

12322

emphasis on rim
or turning part

axle, 'holding
back' part

1232B

UR₂ = limb, base, root
(perhaps the lynchpin)

122FA   TAK₄ = hold back

Axle

Lynchpin

Hub

Spoke

Felloes

12323 UMUM, SIMUG [396x] = metalworker, smith [*cf. True Etym.* *simug => smith*] | umun₂ [16x] = knowledge source; deep thinking

12324 ~ x KASKAL | DE₂ [702x] = to pour, to winnow

12325 ~ x PA

12326 UN | uĝ₃ (ug₃, un) = [704x] **people**, KALAM = The Land (of Sumer)

cpd ùĝ sag gig.ga = Black Sumerians

12327 UN *gunu*

12328 UR = dog; ecstatic [cf. city of UR] | cpd NIG ~ MUG + UR = bitch

12329 UR +-ing UR; 1232A UR *sheshig*

1232B UR₂ = phallus (male cf. MUG, MUNUS vagina, vulva) loin limb, root, base

UR₂ Variants

1232C ~ x A + HA; 1232D ~ x A + NA ; 1232E ~ x AL; 1232F ~ x HA; 12330 ~ x NUN; 12331 ~ x U2; 12332 ~ x U2 + ASH; 12333 ~ x U2 + BI

12334 UR₄ [612x] = to pluck; to gather, collect; to harvest

12335 URI, BUR/BUR = [17x] vessel; 12335 uri-ke = Agade / Akkad [~ + 121A4 KE₄ open field]

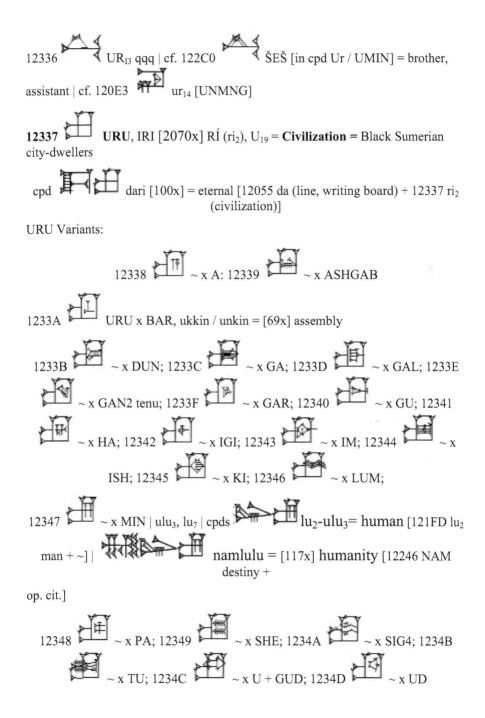

12336 UR₁₃ qqq | cf. 122C0 ŠEŠ [in cpd Ur / UMIN] = brother, assistant | cf. 120E3 ur₁₄ [UNMNG]

12337 **URU**, IRI [2070x] RÍ (ri₂), U₁₉ = **Civilization** = Black Sumerian city-dwellers

cpd dari [100x] = eternal [12055 da (line, writing board) + 12337 ri₂ (civilization)]

URU Variants:

12338 ~ x A: 12339 ~ x ASHGAB

1233A URU x BAR, ukkin / unkin = [69x] assembly

1233B ~ x DUN; 1233C ~ x GA; 1233D ~ x GAL; 1233E ~ x GAN2 tenu; 1233F ~ x GAR; 12340 ~ x GU; 12341 ~ x HA; 12342 ~ x IGI; 12343 ~ x IM; 12344 ~ x ISH; 12345 ~ x KI; 12346 ~ x LUM;

12347 ~ x MIN | ulu₃, lu₇ | cpds lu₂-ulu₃= human [121FD lu₂ man + ~] | namlulu = [117x] humanity [12246 NAM destiny + op. cit.]

12348 ~ x PA; 12349 ~ x SHE; 1234A ~ x SIG4; 1234B ~ x TU; 1234C ~ x U + GUD; 1234D ~ x UD

1234E  URU x URUDA, banshur / banšur = [256x] **table**

..

1234F URUDA, urud [992x] = copper | dab₆ = [30x] go around | determinative &urud; copper / bronze

12350 URUDA x U, TABIRA = copper

12351 USH, **UŠ**, nita, nitaḫ = [2267x] man, male, phallus | ĝeš₃ (ĝiš₃) / gesh = phallus | [312x] unit of length | us₂ (uš) [9695x] = to accompany / follow / adjacent; of a lesser quality; to drag; to stretch; a qualification of grain; to thresh (grain) by treading; to coagulate? | us₂ [4087x] = side, edge; path | us₂ [109x] = to lean on, impose; to check | determinative &m; before male names

[PLM] The Sumerian sign (Jaritz #424), depicts a 'phallus with scrotum. Its main reading is uš (for *ûš), which means 'cohabit, impregnate, stud-animal', representing 'surround-excrete'. The Sumerian word can be found in PIE (Proto-Indo-European): *wes-, 'dampen, wet, male animal', and *wegw-, 'damp, sprinkle'.

cpds

ĝeš₃-dug₄ [46x] = mating [~ + 12157 dug₄ perform]

ĝeš₃-du₃ (/KAK) = mating [~ + 12195 du₃ perform]

ĝeš₃-zig (12363) = erection [~ + 12363 zig rise]

MU-USH (mu-uš) = 60 variant; erection??

ĝeš₃-sur = piss, masturbate [~ + 122E9 sur squeeze / milk]

IM-MA-NI-IN-KA/dug₄ = mating [1214E IM storm + 12220 MA flow + 1224C NI quiver + 12154 IN = abuse, rape + 12157 dug4 / KA = perform, mating]

12352 ~ x A; 12353 ~ x KU; 12354 ~ x KUR; 12355 ~ x TAK4

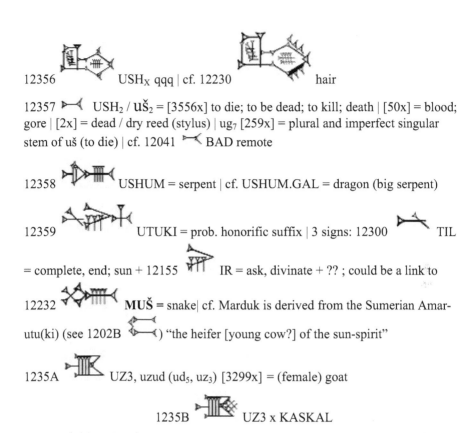

12356 USH_x qqq | cf. 12230 hair

12357 USH₂ / uŠ₂ = [3556x] to die; to be dead; to kill; death | [50x] = blood; gore | [2x] = dead / dry reed (stylus) | ug₇ [259x] = plural and imperfect singular stem of uš (to die) | cf. 12041 BAD remote

12358 USHUM = serpent | cf. USHUM.GAL = dragon (big serpent)

12359 UTUKI = prob. honorific suffix | 3 signs: 12300 TIL = complete, end; sun + 12155 IR = ask, divinate + ?? ; could be a link to

12232 MUŠ = snake| cf. Marduk is derived from the Sumerian Amar-utu(ki) (see 1202B) "the heifer [young cow?] of the sun-spirit"

1235A UZ3, uzud (ud₅, uz₃) [3299x] = (female) goat

1235B UZ3 x KASKAL

1235C UZU [274x] = flesh cf. SIG+UZU hit + flesh = TUD to beat / whip | determinative &uzu; body parts

1235D ZA, **LIMMU₅** [11x] = **4** ["4" four numeric; cf. more used 121F9 limmu₂ [1759x] | NIGIDA LIMMU, DIŠ/DIŠ+DIŠ/DIŠ | ZA = [113x] man; [43x] bead, gem; [113x] CVVE | cpd ZA-E = you [~ + 1208A E interjection]

1235E ZA *tenu* | ad4 [5x] = crippled

1235F ZA sq x KUR

12360 ZAG, ZA₃ [902x] = side; arm; shoulder; border, boundary, district; limit; right side, the right

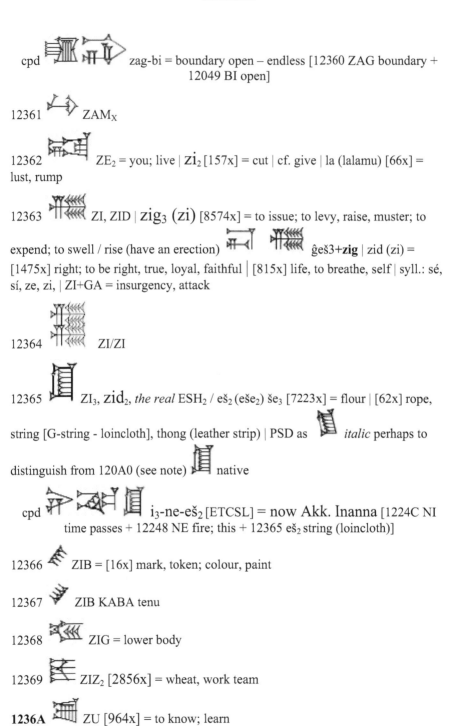

cpd zag-bi = boundary open – endless [12360 ZAG boundary + 12049 BI open]

12361 ZAM$_X$

12362 ZE$_2$ = you; live | zi$_2$ [157x] = cut | cf. give | la (lalamu) [66x] = lust, rump

12363 ZI, ZID | zig$_3$ (zi) [8574x] = to issue; to levy, raise, muster; to expend; to swell / rise (have an erection) ĝeš3+zig | zid (zi) = [1475x] right; to be right, true, loyal, faithful | [815x] life, to breathe, self | syll.: sé, sí, ze, zi, | ZI+GA = insurgency, attack

12364 ZI/ZI

12365 ZI$_3$, zid$_2$, *the real* ESH$_2$ / eš$_2$ (eše$_2$) še$_3$ [7223x] = flour | [62x] rope, string [G-string - loincloth], thong (leather strip) | PSD as *italic* perhaps to distinguish from 120A0 (see note) native

cpd i$_3$-ne-eš$_2$ [ETCSL] = now Akk. **Inanna** [1224C NI time passes + 12248 NE fire; this + 12365 eš$_2$ string (loincloth)]

12366 ZIB = [16x] mark, token; colour, paint

12367 ZIB KABA tenu

12368 ZIG = lower body

12369 ZIZ$_2$ [2856x] = wheat, work team

1236A ZU [964x] = to know; learn

cpds 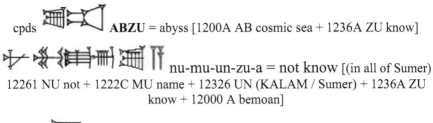 **ABZU** = abyss [1200A AB cosmic sea + 1236A ZU know]

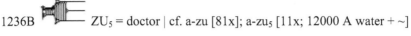 nu-mu-un-zu-a = not know [(in all of Sumer)
12261 NU not + 1222C MU name + 12326 UN (KALAM / Sumer) + 1236A ZU
know + 12000 A bemoan]

1236B  ZU$_5$ = doctor | cf. a-zu [81x]; a-zu$_5$ [11x; 12000 A water + ~]

1236C 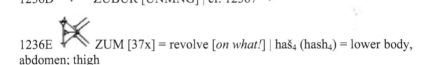 ZU5 x A

1236D ![img] ZUBUR [UNMNG] | cf. 12367 ![img]

1236E ![img] ZUM [37x] = revolve [on what!] | haš$_4$ (hash$_4$) = lower body,
abdomen; thigh

[END]

Mugsar 4-WAY

1. unicode 2. sign 3. lemma 4. translation [28x12013CT]

▷ Sumerians – Kings of the Earthlings

▷ Sumerians called themselves "black-headed people"

▷ There in the tablets, "black people" are the "city-dwellers" and "rulers of Sumer"

▷ First Professors are Black!

▷ Inanna and the Seven Cosmic Powers of her Loincloth

▷ Ninĝirsu's Temple (Gudea Cylinders)

Sumerians – Kings of the Earthlings

Firstly, the issue over the more correct cuneiform. Clearly, it make much more sense that 'gi' 12100 *reed stylus* (writing => knowledge => power; reed marsh of Tigris and Euphrates delta) should be the one we use. Rather than the much less used non-Sumerian, later Babylonian 'gir$_{15}$' 120A0 (local), as shown at PSD for the individual logogram, 4900x to 7x, and the compound for Sumerian language 'eme.gi' 21x over 'eme.gir$_{15}$' only 1x, in the older period. And similarly for tablets refering to the King of Sumer, mainly use ⬦🏹 🏛 'ki.en.gi', rather than ki.en.gir$_{15}$ e.g. the famous Ur-Nammu tablet (see below, also ETCSL, e.g.1: Poem Išme-Dagan (c.2.5.4.01), line c25401.A.364; e.g.2: "Then the Martu peoples, who know no agriculture, arose in all Sumer...", c1822.369). So why do the elites misquote the cuneiform sign actually used?!

Also see Proto Language Monosyllables – Patrick Ryan clearly knows what he is talking about, "...*Emegi*, the language of males in Sumer, differs in some interesting ways from equivalent forms in *Emesal*, the language of females..."

gi [REED] (4900x: ED IIIa, ED IIIb, Old Akkadian, Lagash II, Ur III)
"reed, cane; a unit of length" Akk. *qanû*

𒄑 gi

7000^{CT}/3000^{Pl}	7500 / 2500	8000 / 2000
977	3725	189

ĝir [NATIVE] (7x: Old Babylonian) wr. ĝir$_{15}$ "native, local"

𒄀 ĝir$_{15}$

7000^{CT}/3000^{Pl}	7500 / 2500	8000 / 2000
		7

eme ĝir [SUMERIAN] (32x: Ur III, Old Babylonian) wr. eme-gi; eme-ĝir$_{15}$
"the Sumerian language" Akk. *šumeritum; šumerû*

[1] 𒅴𒄑   eme-gi

[2] 𒅴𒄀   eme-ĝir$_{15}$

	7000 CT 3000 *plag.*	7500 2500	8000 2000
[1]		21	2
[2]		1	8

PSD

[12174 'eme' = tongue, language + 12100 GI reed / write]

One can imagine that the Sumerians were dominant and respected by other states because they could write, hence the emphasis on reed stylus. Thus they were looked on as, "Kings of the Earthlings because the stylus is mightier than the sword".

Tablet of Ur-Nammu

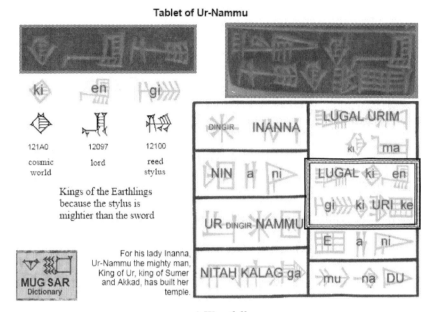

ki	en	gi
121A0	12097	12100
cosmic world	lord	reed stylus

Kings of the Earthlings because the stylus is mightier than the sword

MUG SAR Dictionary

For his lady Inanna, Ur-Nammu the mighty man, King of Ur, king of Sumer and Akkad, has built her temple.

4-Way follows...

Inanna lady (wonder) come to pass Ur-Nammu the mighty man

12239	cpd	12000	1224C	cpd	cpd
ᵈInanna	nin	a	ni	Ur-Nammu	nitaḫ-kalag-ga
Inanna determ. 1202D AN+ 12239 MUŠ₃	lady, mistress 122A9 MUG cuneus + 12306 TUG₂ garment	bemoan / sigh of wonder ; progeny; (water)	comes to pass	(Ur-Engur) 12328 UR dog, city? + determ. 1202D AN+ 121C9 cosmic waters	mighty man 12351 NITAḪ male + 12197 KALAG mighty + 120B5 GA suckling, young

King of Ur, King of **Sumer** and Akkad

cpd	cpd	cpd
lugal ur-im-ki	lugal ki-en-**gi** ki	uri-ke
King of Ur	King of Sumer	and Akkad
12217 LUGAL King + cpd Ur-im + 121A0 KI city	12217 LUGAL King + Sumer: "121A0 KI cosmic world + 12097 EN lord + 12100 GI place of reeds stylus, writing, knowledge, power" + 121A0 KI city	12335 URI vessel, (Akkad) + 121A4 KE_4 open field

..
temple build

cpd	cpd
e-a-ni	mu-na-du
temple	build
1208D E_2 temple + aux a-ni: "12000 A wonder + 1224C NI timelessness"	1222C MU year, name + 1223E NA pestle + 12195 DU build

Sumerians called themselves "black-headed people"

cpd
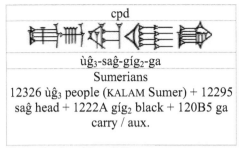
ùĝ₃-saĝ-gíg₂-ga
Sumerians
12326 ùĝ₃ people (KALAM Sumer) + 12295 saĝ head + 1222A gíg₂ black + 120B5 ga carry / aux.

Examples in tablets follow...

There in the tablets, "black people" are the "city-dwellers" and "rulers of Sumer"

(Cont. from Inanna)

231. His father replied to the boy;
232. his father replied to Šukaletuda:
233. "My son, you should join the city-dwellers your brothers the rulers of Sumer.
234. Go at once to the black-headed people, your brothers!
235. Then this woman [Inanna] will not find you in the lands of Sumer."
236. He joined the city-dwellers, his brothers all together.
237. He went at once to the black-headed people, his brothers,
238. and the woman did not find him in the lands.
[ETCSL: c133.231]

231.   lu$_2$-tur ad-da-ni mu-na-ni-ib-gi$_4$-gi$_4$
232.   šu-kal-/le\-tud-da ad-[da-ni] mu-na-ni-ib-gi$_4$-gi$_4$
233.   dumu-ĝu$_{10}$ iri šeš-zu ḫe$_2$-eb-us$_2$-en
234.   saĝ gig$_2$ šeš-zu-ne ĝiri3 gub-ba ĝen-na
235.   munus-e šag4 kur-kur-ra-ka nu-um-ma-ni-in-pad$_3$-de$_3$-en
236.   iri šeš-a-ni ni2-bi-a im-us2
237.   saĝ gig$_2$ šeš-a-ni ĝiri3 gub-ba im-ĝen
238.   munus-e šag4 kur-kur-ra-ka nu-um-ma-ni-in-pad3

4-Way follows...

Inanna & Šukaletuda (c.1.3.3), line c133.231 [cont from Inanna 138b]
231. lu$_2$-tur ad-da-ni mu-na-ni-ib-gi$_4$-gi$_4$
[ETCSL: His father replied to the boy]
son father for a time tossed the problem around

cpd	cpd	cpd
lu$_2$-tur	ad-da-ni	mu-na-ni-ib-gi$_4$-gi$_4$
son	father	tossed the problem around
121FD lu$_2$ male + 12309 TUR son	1201C AD father + 12055 DA line (gen.) + 1224C NI in time	1222C MU year, dear, name, son + 1223E NA pestle + 1224C NI comes to pass + 12141 IB oval + 12104 x2 gi$_4$-gi$_4$ (conversation) reply

etcsl.orinst.ox...c133.231 (or c133.177)

..
232. šu-kal-/le\-tud-da ad-[da-ni] mu-na-ni-ib-gi$_4$-gi$_4$
[ETCSL: his father replied to Šukaletuda]
Šukaletuda father for a time tossed the problem around

cpd closeup	cpd	cpd
šu-kal-le-tud-da	ad-da-ni	mu-na-ni-ib-gi$_4$-gi$_4$
Šukaletuda	father	advised
122D7 ŠU hand + 12197 KAL mighty + 121F7 LE branch + 12305 TU small + 12055 DA line	op. cit.	op. cit.

etcsl.ohinst.ox...c133.232

233. dumu-ĝu10 **iri šeš-zu** ḫe2-eb-us2-**en** [Inanna-Šukaletuda c133.233]
[ETCSL: "My son, you should join the city-dwellers your brothers.]
son **city-dwellers your brothers** get protection from them the **rulers of Sumer**

12309	12337	122C0	cpd
dumu-ĝu$_{10}$	**iri**	**šeš-zu**	ḫe$_2$-eb-us$_2$-**en**
son	city-	brothers	get protection from the rulers
12309 TUR	dwellers	122C0 šeš	of Sumer
son + 1222C		brother +	120F6 ḫe$_2$ be he + 12141 IB
ĝu$_{10}$ dear, son		1236A ZU	oval + 12351 us$_2$ lean on +
		know	12097 EN rulers of Sumer

etcsl.orinst.ox...c133.233

..

234. **saĝ gig2 šeš-zu-ne** ĝiri3 gub-ba ĝen-na [Inanna-Šukaletuda c133.234]
[ETCSL: Go at once to the black-headed people, **your brothers**!]
black people your brothers hop to it go

12295	1222A	122C0|12248	1210A	1207A	cpd
saĝ	**gig$_2$**	**šeš-zu-ne**	ĝiri$_3$	gub-ba	ĝen-na
head /	black	brothers your	foot; path,	stand	go
people		op. cit.	12248	via	1207A	1207A ĝen
		NE these / your		DU stand	go + 1223E
				+ 12040	pestle
				BA split	

etcsl.orinst.ox...c133.234

SUMERIAN CUNEIFORM DICTIONARY

235. munus-e šag4 kur-kur-ra-ka nu-um-ma-ni-in-pad3-de3-en
[ETCSL: Then this woman [Inanna] will not find you in all the lands."]
That woman! interior of all the land talking did not find in Sumer the rapist

122A9	122AE	cpd	cpd
𒐊	◈	𒐊	𒐊
munus-e	šag$_4$	kur-kur-ra-ka	nu-um-ma-ni-in-pad$_3$-de$_3$ EN
That woman! munus + 1208A E interjection	interior	in all the land talking (about the rape) 121B3 KUR lands + 1228F RA aux. + 12157 KA talk	not find in Sumer the rapist (of Inanna) op. cit. pad$_3$. + 12097 EN abbrev. for Sumer

etcsl.orinst.ox...c133.235

236. iri šeš-a-ni ni2-bi-a im-us2
[ETCSL: He joined the city-dwellers, his brothers all together.]
city dwellers his brothers in time all together joined

12337	cpd	cpd	12351
𒐊	𒐊	𒐊	𒐊
iri	šeš-a-ni	ni$_2$-bi-a	im-us$_2$
city-dwellers	brothers his 122C0 šeš brother + 12000 A bemoan + 1224C NI in time	themselves (1224E ni$_2$ + 12049 BI + 12000 A) [see ETCSL]	joined 1214E IM copula+ 12351 us$_2$ accompany, follow

etcsl.orinst.ox...c133.236

237. **saĝ gig2** šeš-a-ni ĝiri3 gub-ba im-ĝen
[ETCSL: He went at once to the black-headed people, his brothers,]
black people his brothers hopping to it went

12295	1222A	cpd	1210A	1207A	cpd
saĝ	gig$_2$	šeš-a-ni	ĝiri$_3$	gub-ba	im-ĝen
head / people	black	brothers his op. cit. 236	foot op. cit. 234	stand op. cit. 234	went 1214E IM copula + 1207A ĝen go

etcsl.orinst.ox...c133.237

..

238. munus-e šag4 kur-kur-ra-ka nu-um-ma-ni-in-pad3
[ETCSL: and the woman did not find him in the land.]
That woman! interior of all the land did not find the rapist

122A9	122AE	cpd	cpd
munus-e	šag$_4$	kur-kur-ra-ka	nu-um-ma-ni-in-pad$_3$
That woman! op. cit. 235	interior	in the land op. cit.	not find the rapist (of Inanna) op. cit. pad$_3$.

etcsl.orinst.ox...c133.238
[END extract] | 231 | 4-Way top | TOC2

ETCSL Search: **"black-headed people"** saĝ-gig2 (-ga)

4-Way top | Very Common Signs | TOC2

137-148. The francolin ...... to the ...... of its .... The francolin ...... to the birthplace of Dumuzid. Like a pigeon on its window ledge it took counsel with itself; the francolin in its shelter took counsel. Only his mother Durtur can gladden my master! Only his mother Durtur can gladden Dumuzid! My goddess, born in Kuara, the maiden who is the crown of all ......, the admiration and acclaim of **the black-headed people**, the playful one who also voices laments and the cries, who intercedes before the king -- Ĝeštin-ana, the lady, did ....

..

137.   [...]-ba-še3 buru5-ḫabrudmušen-e nam /il2\

138.   ki-ulutim2 ddumu-zid-da-še3 buru5-ḫabrudmušen-e [...]

139.   tum12mušen-gin7 ab-lal3-ba ni2-bi-a ad-e-eš ba-ni-ib2-gi4

140.   buru5-ḫabrudmušen-e a2-bur2-ba ad-e-eš ba-ni-ib-gi4

141.   lugal-ĝu10 ama-ni ddur7-/tur\-ra-am3 i3-ḫul2-le

142.   ddumu-zid-de3 ama-ni <ddur7-tur-ra-am3 i3-ḫul2-le>

143.   in-nin-ĝu10 u3-tud-da kuaraki

144.   ki-sikil amar sig7-ga men-bi

145.   u6 di niĝ2-me-ĝar **saĝ gig2-ga**

146.   e-ne dug4-dug4 i-lu akkil dug4-dug4

147.   nam-šita dug4-dug4 lugal-la [...]

148.   dĝeštin-an-na-ke4 nin [...]

--

c.1.3.2/Tr/Gl   saĝ gig2-ga šir3-re-eš bi2-ib-ra

She shall determine fates. She shall apportion the divine powers among the Anuna, the great gods. And as for you, I will place in your hands the lives of **the black-headed people**." When you get there, let the woman I have chosen for her beauty ...... her mother. Do not go to her empty-handed, but take her some jewellery in your left hand. Waste no time. Return with her answer quickly."

--

31-38. In the Gagiššua of the great palace, where she renders verdicts with grandeur, he made the great mother Ninlil glad. Enlil and Ninlil relished it there. In its great dining hall, the trustworthy hero chosen by Nunamnir made them enjoy a magnificent meal: the E-kur was rejoicing. They looked with approval at the shepherd Ur-Namma, and the Great Mountain decreed a great destiny for **Ur-Nammu** for all time, making him the mightiest among his **black-headed people**.

31.   ĝa2-ĝiš-šu2-a /e2\-gal maḫ-di gal ku5-ru-da-ni

32.   /ama\ gal dnin-lil2-ra ul mu-na-ni-in-de6

33.   den-lil2 dnin-lil2-bi dug3 mi-ni-in-ĝal2-le-eš

34.   unu2 gal-ba šul zid mu pad3-da dnu-nam-nir-ra-ka (zi-kir šu-mi)

35.   ninda maḫ am3-mi-ni-dug3 e2-kur ḫul2-la-am3

36.   igi zid mu-un-ši-in-bar-re-eš sipad dur-dnamma-ra

37.   kur gal-e sipad dur-dnamma-ra nam gal ud su3-ra2-še3 mu-ni-in-tar

38.   **saĝ gig2-ga**-na a2 mi-ni-in-maḫ

--

4-Way top | Very Common Signs | TOC2

ETCSL translation : t.2.5.3.4

http://etcsl.orinst.ox...c.2.5.3.4

A šir-namerima (?) for Iddin-Dagan (Iddin-Dagan D)

1-2. Great lady, majestic physician to **the black-headed**, holy Ninisina, daughter of An, may you be praised!

3-9. Lady whose tempest, like a raging storm, ... the interior of heaven and the trembling earth, whose upraised fierce face, like a fire, rips the bodies of the enemy; who, like a dragon, does not bring up venom in her place where ......, paws of a lion, sharpened knives, claws constantly dripping blood, ... which prick the body with fear! When you draw through the flesh the scalpel and the lancet, knives like lion's claws -- the bodies of **the black-headed people** tremble because of you!

..

1.   nin gal <a>-zu maḫ **saĝ gig2-ga**

2.   kug dnin-isin2si-na dumu an-na me-teš2 ḫe2-i-i

3.   nin tum9u18-lu-ni ud mir-a-gin7 an-šag4-a ki? dub2-bu X

4.   dgibil6-gin7 igi /ḫuš il2\-la-ni erim2-ma su dar-dar-re

5.   ušumgal-gin7 ki KA X-a-na uš11-bi nu-ed3-de3

6.   /šu piriĝ\-ĝa2 ĝiri2 u3-sar ak umbin uš2 biz-biz-biz

7.   su X ḪA E de2-de3 ni2 su-a ru-ru-gu2

8.   ĝiri2-zal bulug-kiĝ2-gur4 ĝiri2 piriĝ-ĝa2-gin7 uzu e3-a-zu-uš

9.   **uĝ3 saĝ gig2** su ma-ra-sag3-sag3-ge

--

A praise poem of Ḥammu-rābi (Ḥammu-rābi A)

http://etcsl.orinst.ox...c.2.8.2.1

1-17.

1 line fragmentary ...... acting as its lord ......

7 lines fragmentary ...... **the black-headed** .... the Euphrates ....
the Tigris ....

10.   [...]-zu X um-ma-ri **saĝ gig2-ga** [(...)] /IM?\ en GIL

--

http://etcsl.orinst.ox...c.5.5.4

18-27. Here, {in {'Where Flesh Came Forth'} {(1 ms. has instead:) 'Where Flesh
Grew'} (the name of a cosmic location), he set this very hoe (al) to work;} {(1 other
ms. has instead:) in 'Where Flesh Grew' the unassailable (?),} he had it place the
first model of mankind in the brick mould. His Land started to break through the
soil towards Enlil. He looked with favour at his black-headed people. Now the
Anuna gods stepped forward to him, and did (ĝal) obeisance to him. They calmed
Enlil with a prayer, for they wanted to demand (al-dug) **the black-headed people**
from him. Ninmena, the lady who had given birth to the ruler, who had given birth
to the king, now set (alĝaĝa) human reproduction going.

..

18.   {{uzu-e3-a} {(1 ms. has instead:) uzu-mu2-a} ĝišal am3-mi-ni-in-du3}

{

(1 other ms. has instead the line:)

18A.   uzu-mu2-a saĝ nu-ĝa2-ĝa2-de3

}

19.   saĝ nam-lu2-ulu3 u3-šub-ba mi-ni-in-ĝar

20.   den-lil2-še3 kalam-ma-ni ki mu-un-ši-in-dar-re

21.   saĝ gig2-ga-ni-še3 igi zid mu-ši-in-bar

22.   da-nun-na mu-un-na-sug2-sug2-ge-eš

23.   šu-bi giri17-ba mu-un-ne-ĝal2

24.   den-lil2 a-ra-zu-a mu-ni-in-ḫuĝ-e-ne

25.   **uĝ3 saĝ gig2-ga** al mu-un-da-be2-ne

26.   nin en u3-tud-de3 lugal u3-tud-de3

27.   dnin-men-na-ke4 tud-tud al-ĝa2-ĝa2

--

etcsl.orinst.ox...c.5.3.6

1-10.

2 lines fragmentary of Enlil .... Small ten-**shekel** pieces of silver ......

6 lines fragmentary ... unknown no. of lines missing

1-11.

5 lines fragmentary ...... in aromatic oil of cedar .... humans, **the black-headed people**. Let him anoint each with my ...... aromatic oil of cedar. ...... it is an abomination to my king.

..

7.   [...] /lu2\-ulu3 **uĝ3 saĝ gig2**-ge

8.   [...] i3 šim ĝišerin-na-ĝa2-ta-am3 ḫa-mu-ta-/šeš4\-e

9.   [...] ḪI-bi-ra lugal-ĝa2 niĝ2-gig-bi-[im]

--

Sumer

The Victory of Utu-Hengal, ETCSL transliteration : c.2.1.6.

4. ki-en-gi-ra2 nij2-a-erim2 /bi2-in\-si-a

21. sig-ce3 ki-en-gi-ra2 {gana2} {(1 ms. has instead:) jic} bi2-kece2

http://etcsl.orinst.ox.ac.uk...c533.236

236-247. "When the šem and ala drums, ... and other instruments play together for him, he passes the time with your heart-gladdening tigi and zamzam instruments. But it is I who have made the wine plentiful and made much to eat and drink. I perfect the garments with fine oil. I bring up the ......, the šutur and aktum garments. As for safeguarding, the best in **Sumer**, in the oppressive heat (?) of Summer, where they had been put away in the bedrooms amongst **the black-headed people**, moths destroy the blankets and make the aktum cloth perish because of you. ...... exhausts itself for you .... The wooden chest .... I am Ninkasi's help, for her I sweeten the beer, with as much cold water, the tribute of the hills, as you brought."

..

236.   šem3 kuša2-la2 si-ŠIR3 ĝiš-gu3-di ni2-ba u3-mu-na-du12

237.   tigi za-am-za-am niĝ2 šag4 ḫul2-la-zu ud mi-ni-ib-zal-zal-e

238.   ĝe26-e ĝeštin lu-lu-me-en gu7 naĝ gal-gal-me-en

239.   tug2 i3 dug3-ge ba-ab-du7-me-en

240.   /niĝ2\-tug2-ba tug2šutur tug2aktum-ma a2 ba-ni-e3-a-me-en

241.   /kum2\-ma dugud e2-me-eš **saĝ ki-en-gi*-ra** zi-bi tum2-tum2-de3

242. **uĝ3 saĝ gig2-ga** ur2-bi-a ki-nu2 ĝar-ĝar-ra-bi

243. tug2niĝ2-barag2 nim mu-ra-be4-be4 tug2aktum mu-ra-saḫ6

244. ĝišniĝ2-keše2-da a2 mu-ra-ab-kuš2-u3 e2-gal ma-ra-ŠEŠ-ŠEŠ

245. ĝišgu2-ne-saĝ-ĝa2-ke4 mu-un-kiĝ2-kiĝ2 en3 tar mu-ni-ĝal2

246. dnin-ka-si-ke4 a2-taḫ-a-ni-me-en kaš mu-un-na-ab-dug3-ge-en

247. a sed4 gu2-un ḫur-saĝ-ĝa2 a-na mu-e-tum2-tum2-mu

* So here in one of the few extant examples, 'Sumer' = "saĝ ki-en-gi"
= head(/people) +
cosmic world + lord + *reed stylus* 'gi' [not little used 'gir₁₅' *native*]

[END Black Sumerians]

First Professors are Black!
The advice of a supervisor to a younger scribe (E-dub-ba-a C)
(*The supervisor speaks:*)
1. dumu e$_2$-dub-ba-a ud ul-la ĝa$_2$-nu ki-ĝu$_{10}$-še$_3$
[ETCSL: {Apprentice!} One-time member of the school, come here to me,]
Apprentice scribe school once supervised won't you come down to the designated place

12309	cpd	12313	1230C+121B7	120B7+12261	cpd
dumu	e$_2$-dub-ba-a	UD	ul-la	ĝa$_2$-nu	ki-ĝu$_{10}$-še$_3$
appren -tice	scribe school 1208D e$_2$ school, house + 1207E DUB tablet + 12040 BA allot, share + 12000 progeny	day, once...	distant time + show, supervise	place, come down + NU not (won't you come)	designated place 121A0 KI place + 1222C MU name son + 12365 še$_3$ string

Note: Original translation inexplicably doesn't bother to translate the very first word, "dumu" = apprentice – probably the most interesting and important part of the whole introduction...
http://etcsl.orinst.ox....c513.1

2. niĝ$_2$ **um-mi**-a-ĝu$_{10}$ mu-un-pad$_3$-da za-e ga-ra-pad$_3$-pad$_3$
http://etcsl.orinst.ox...c513.2
[ETCSL: and let me explain to you what my teacher revealed]
something, dear **professor, who of course must be black,** revealed to the people of
Sumer, you, like threshing grain will be revealed

120FB	cpd	cpd	cpd	cpd
niĝ$_2$	um-mi-a-ĝu$_{10}$	mu-un-pad$_3$-da	za-e	ga-ra-pad$_3$-pad$_3$
some-thing	**professor who of course must be black** 1231D UM reed stem (stylus / writing symbol) (1207E tablet var) + 1222A MI black* + 12000 progeny + 1222C ĝu$_{10}$ dear	revealed to the people of Sumer 1222C MU name + 12326 UN (KALAM = Sumer) + cpd pad$_3$ reveal + 12055 DA writing board	you 1235D + 1208A	like threshing grain will be revealed 120B5 GA bring + 1228F RA threshing + cpd pad$_3$ reveal x2

* There are some who say that when the Sumerians call themselves black it should not be taken literally, and black means local or something. Also in signs for other professions the scribes don't add this extra point, but here they emphasize the first professors that started the education revolution 5000 years ago are BLACK!

ummia [EXPERT] (142x: ED IIIb, Old Akkadian, Ur III

expert, master craftsman

um-mi-a

Not just the Sumerians calling themselves black, the first professors are BLACK!

7000CT/5000ya	7500CT/4500ya	8000CT/4000ya
14	110	18

PSD

3. za-e-gin$_7$-nam nam-lu$_2$-tur i$_3$-ak šeš-gal i$_3$-tuku-am$_3$
[ETCSL: "Like you, I was once a youth and had a mentor]

za-e-gin$_7$-nam	nam-lu$_2$-tur	i$_3$-ak	šeš-gal	i$_3$-tuku-am$_3$
you (sg.)	status as child	to do	elder	to have
ZA-E-DIM$_2$-NAM	NAM-LU$_2$-TUR	NI-AK	brother	NI-TUK-A.AN
			ŠEŠ-GAL	

http://etcsl.orinst.ox.c513.3
END current WIP

3-8.

"Like you, I was once a youth and had a mentor.

The teacher assigned a task to me -- it was man's work.

Like a springing reed, I leapt up and put myself to work.

I did not depart from my teacher's instructions,
and I did not start doing things on my own initiative.

My mentor was delighted with my work on the assignment.

He rejoiced that I was humble before him and he spoke in my favour."

3.za-e-gin7-nam nam-lu2-tur i3-ak šeš-gal i3-tuku-am3

4. um-mi-a lu2-ta kiĝ2-ĝa2-am3 a2 aĝ2-ĝa2 ĝiš bi2-in-ĝar

5. gi al-gu4-ud-da-gin7 i3-gu4-ud-de3-en kiĝ2-ĝa2 bi2-in-sig10-ge-en

6. inim um-mi-a-ĝu10 nu-un-taka4 niĝ2 ni2-ĝa2 li-bi2-ak

7. šeš-gal-ĝu10 a2 ĝiš ĝar-ra-ĝa2 šag4-ga-ni i-ni-in-dug3

8. i3-sun5-ne na-mu-da-ši-ḫul2 silim-ĝa2 i-ni-in-dug4

9-15.
 9. "I just did whatever he outlined for me -- everything was always in its place.
10. Only a fool would have deviated from his instructions.

11. He guided my hand on the clay and kept me on the right path.

12. He made me eloquent with words and gave me advice.

13. He focused my eyes on the rules which guide a man with a task:
14. zeal is proper for a task, time-wasting is taboo;
15. anyone who wastes time on his task is neglecting his task."

 9. ĝiš ma-an-ḫur-ra na-an-dim2 ki-bi-še3 al-ĝar-ĝar

10. na de5-ga-ni-ta lu2 ḫu-ru-um šu bar dib-ba-e

11. im-ma šu-ĝu10 si ba-ni-in-sa2 us2 zid mu-un-dab5

12. ka-ĝu10 inim-ma ĝal2 ba-ni-in-taka4 ad gi4-gi4 ma-an-pad3

13. ĝiš-ḫur lu2 a2 aĝ2-ĝa2 si sa2-e igi ma-ni-in-si-si

14. gu2 zi-zi-i ḫa-la a2 aĝ2-ĝa2-kam ud zal-le niĝ2-gig-ga

15. lu2 ki a2 aĝ2-ĝa2-ni-še3 ud zal-la a2 aĝ2-ĝa2-ni ab-taka4

16-20.
"He did not vaunt his knowledge: his words were modest.

If he had vaunted his knowledge, people would have frowned.

Do not waste time, do not rest at night -- get on with that work!

Do not reject the pleasurable company of a mentor or his assistant:

once you have come into contact with such great brains,
you will make your own words more worthy."

16. niĝ2-zu-a-ni pa nu-um-e3 ka-ga14-ni ba-an-la2

17. tukum-bi niĝ2-zu-a-ni pa ba-an-e3 igi mu-un-suḫ-suḫ-u3-ne

18. ud na-ab-zal-e-en ĝi6 na-ab-sed4-e-en a2-bi-še3 ĝen-na

19. šeš-gal šeš-ban3-da ḫi-li-a-bi na-an-na-ni-ib-gi4-gi4

20. saĝ-ki gal-gal-la um-ma-te inim-zu ba-dugud-de3-en

21-26.
*"And another thing: you will never return to your blinkered vision;
that would be greatly to demean due deference, the decency of
mankind.*

Worthy plants [offerings?] calm the heart, and sins are absolved.

An empty-handed man's gifts are respected as such.

Even a poor man clutches a kid to his chest as he kneels.

*You should defer to the powers that be and ...... -- that will calm
you."*

21. 2-kam-ma-še3 igi keše2-da-zu-še3 nu-ra-ni-ib-gi4-gi4

22. ki za-za teš2 lu2-u18-lu-ka maḫ-bi gu2 ḫe2-ri-du3

23. u2 teš2-a-ka šag4 ab-sed4-de3 nam-tag-ga al-du8-e

24. lu2 šu sug4-ga-ka kadra-ni ur5-še3 nir mu-un-ĝal2

25. lu2 niĝ2 nu-tuku maš2 gur-ra-na gaba-na i-im-tab

26. lu2-ĝarza2-ra ki ḫe2-en-ne-za ḫe2-keše2 ba-sed4-de3

27-28.
"There, I have recited to you what my teacher revealed, and you will not neglect it.

You should pay attention -- taking it to heart will be to your benefit!"

27. niĝ2 um-mi-a-ĝu10 mu-un-pad3-de3 e-ra-šid nu-mu-ra-ab-taka4

28. ĝizzal ḫe2-bi2-ak šag4-še3 gid2-i-de3 sag9-ge-zu mu-da-an-ĝal2

29-35.
The learned scribe humbly answered his supervisor:

"I shall give you a response to what you have just recited like a magic spell,
and a rebuttal to your charming ditty delivered in a bellow.

Do not make me out to be an ignoramus -- I will answer you once and for all!
You opened my eyes like a puppy's and you made me into a human being.

But why do you go on outlining rules for me as if I were a shirker?

Anyone hearing your words would feel insulted!"

29. dub-sar umun2 ak sun5-na-bi ugula-a-ni mu-un-na-ni-ib-gi4-gi4

30. ud mu7-mu7-gin7 ab-šid-en-na-a ba-an-gi4-bi a-ra-ab-ḫa-za-an

31. mu gud-gin7 i-lu dug3-ga-zu-še3 ĝiš i3-la2-a-bi

32. lu2 nu-zu nam-mu-ni-ib-ku4-ku4 1(DIŠ)-am3 ga-ra-ni-ib-gi4
(1 ms. inserts lines 60A and 60B here instead of after line 60)

33. ur-gir15 tur-gin7 igi mu-e-bad-bad nam-lu2-ulu3 mu-e-ak

34. a-na-aš-am3 lu2 ĝa2-la dag-ga-gin7 ĝiš ma-ab-ḫur-ḫur-re-en

35. lu2 inim-zu ĝiš ba-ni-in-tuku-a šu am3-ma-kar2-kar2

36-41.

"Whatever you revealed of the scribal art has been repaid to you.

You put me in charge of your household and I have never served you by shirking.

I have assigned duties to the slave girls, slaves and subordinates in your household.

I have kept them happy with rations, clothing and oil rations,
and I have assigned the order of their duties to them,
so that you do not have to follow the slaves around in the house of their master.

I do this as soon as I wake up, and I chivvy them around like sheep."

36. nam-dub-sar-ra a-na mu-e-pad3-da-zu šu-za ba-ni-in-šum2

37. e2-za ḫe2-bi2-gub-be2-en ud na-me niĝ2 ĝa2-la dag-ga-ĝu10-uš sa2 ba-ra-am3-mu-ri-ib-dug4

38. geme2 arad2 ĝiri3-sig10-ga e2-za kiĝ2-gi4-a ḫe2-bi2-ne-gi4

39. šukur2-bi tug2-bi u3 i3-ba-bi šag4-bi ḫa-ma-dug3-ga

40. a-ra2-bi-še3 kiĝ2-gi4-a ḫe2-bi2-in-ne-gi4 e2 lugal-ka arad2 ba-ra-bi2-in-us2

41. gaba ud-ĝa2 ḫe2-bi2-ak udu-gin7 ḫe2-eb-us2-u3-nam

42-49.

"When you have ordered offerings to be prepared, I have performed them for you on the appropriate days.

43] I have made the sheep and banquets attractive, so that your god is overjoyed.

44] When the boat of your god arrives, people should greet it with respect.

45] When you have ordered me to the edge of the fields, I have made the men work there.

It is challenging work which permits no sleep either at night or in the heat of day, if the cultivators are to do their best at the field-borders.

I have restored quality to your fields, so people admire you.

Whatever your task for the oxen, I have exceeded it and have fully completed their loads for you."

42. sizkur2 sa gi4-gi4-da ḫe2-mu-e-dug4 ud-bi sa2 ḫe2-ri-ib-dug4

43. udu-bi u2-gu7-bi ḫa-ma-sag9-sag9 diĝir-zu ḫe2-ḫul2

44. ud ma2 diĝir-za us2-sa-bi giri17 šu ḫa-ra-ab-tag-ge-ne

45. gaba a-šag4-ga-še3 a2 ḫe2-mu-e-da-a-a-aĝ2 erin2-e kiĝ2 ḫe2-bi2-ak

46. kiĝ2 a-da-min3-na ĝi6 an-bar7-ba u3 ba-ra-bi2-ku-am3

47. us2-a-DU dumu engar-ra-ke4-e-ne saĝ ḫu-mu-un-kal-le-ne

48. a-šag4-za šu nam-sag9-ga ḫe2-bi2-gi4 uĝ3-e u6 di ḫe2-ri-ib-dug4

49. gud-de3 a-na-am3 gub-zu dirig ḫe2-em-tum3 gu2-un-bi ḫa-ra-ab-silim-ma-am3

50-53.
"Since my childhood you have scrutinised me and kept an eye on my behaviour,
inspecting it like fine silver -- there is no limit to it!

Without speaking grandly -- as is your shortcoming -- I serve before you.

But those who undervalue themselves are ignored by you -- know that I want to make this clear to you."

50. tur-ra-ĝu10-ta ḫe2-em-ma-dim4-e-en a-ra2-ĝu10 igi ḫe2-bi2-du8

51. kug sag9-ga-gin7 kurum7 ḫe2-bi2-ak ki-šer11 la-ba-an-tuku

52. gal-bi nu-di niĝ2-gig-zu-gin7 e-ra-da-tuš-u3-nam

53. ni2 tur-tur-re e-ra-da-saḫ6-saḫ6-na pa ga-ra-ab-e3 zu-a

54-59. (The supervisor answers:)
"Raise your head now, you who were formerly a youth.
You can turn your hand against any man, so act as is befitting."
(The scribe speaks:)
"Through you who offered prayers and so blessed me,
who instilled instruction into my body as if I were consuming milk and butter,
who showed his service to have been unceasing,
I have experienced success and suffered no evil."

54. ud-bi-ta lu2-tur ḫe2-me-en-na i3-ne-eš2 saĝ-zu il2

55. šu-zu lu2-ra mu-da-an-gi4-gi4-in a-ra2-bi-še3 DU-mu-un

56. šudu3 ḫe2-mu-e-ša4 nam mu-tar-ra

57. na de5-ga ga i3 gu7-a-gin7 su-ĝa2 i-ni-in-kur9-ra

58. gub-bu ĝa2-la nu-dag-ge pad3-da-zu

59. ki sag9-ga-bi sa2 ḫe2-ri-ib-dug4 niĝ2-ḫul-bi li-bi2-in-ak

60-61. (The supervisor answers:)
"The teachers, those learned men, should value you highly.
{(2 mss. add 3 lines, 1 of the 2 mss. adds 2 more lines which
corresponds to lines 67 and 68 in this edition:)
They should ... in their houses and in prominent places.
Your name will be hailed as honourable for its prominence.
For your sweet songs even the cowherds will strive gloriously.
For your sweet songs I too shall strive and shall ...
The teacher will bless you with a joyous heart.}
You who as a youth sat at my words have pleased my heart."

60. um-mi-a lu2 inim zu-u3-ne saĝ ḫu-mu-un-kal-le-ne

   {2 mss. add 3 lines:)

60A. e2-bi-a ki saĝ-kal-la-ba DI-DI ḫu-mu-un-e-ne

60B. mu-zu dug3-ge-eš pad3-de3-da-bi saĝ-ki-bi ma-ĝal2
   (1 of the 2 mss. has lines 67 and 68 after line 60B instead of after
line 66)

60E. um-mi-a šag4 ḫul2-la-ni-ta šudu3 mu-na-an-ša4

61. lu2-tur inim-ĝu10-še3 ba-tuš-u3-nam šag4-ĝu10 bi2-dug3-ga-am3

62-72.
"Nisaba has placed in your hand the honour of being a teacher.
{For her, the fate determined for you will be changed and so you will
be generously blessed}
{(1 ms. has instead:)

You were created by Nisaba! May you ... upwards}.
May she bless you with a joyous heart and free you from all
despondency. ...
at whatever is in the school, the place of learning.

66] The majesty of Nisaba ... silence.
For your sweet songs even the cowherds will strive gloriously.

For your sweet songs I too shall strive and shall ....[omitted: 'do
something for your MUNUS']

They should recognise that you are a practitioner (?) of wisdom.

The little fellows should enjoy like beer the sweetness of decorous
words:
experts bring light to dark places, they bring it to culs-de-sac and
streets."

62. dnisaba dugud-da um-mi-a šu-za i-ni-in-ĝar-ra

63. {nam i-ri-tar-ra mu-na-ra-kur2-ru šu zid ḫa-ra-an-ĝa2-ĝa2}
    {(1 ms. has instead the line:)
    šu dug4-ga dnisaba-me-en gu2 an-še3 [...]}

64. šag4 ḫul2-la nam-še3 ḫe2-bi2-tar šag4 sag3 ḫe2-da-zig3

65. e2-dub-ba-a ki-umum-ma a-na ĝal2-la [...]

66. nam-maḫ dnisaba niĝ2-me-ĝar pad3-pad3 di-da-/bi?

67. gud-us2 šir3 dug₃-dug₃-ga-zu-še3 ĝiš la2-bi maḫ

68. šir3 dug₃-ga-zu-še3 ĝiš ga-mu-ni-in-la2 MUNUS-zu-gin7 ga-mu-
    ni-tag-tag

69. niĝ2 ĝeštug2-ga nu-u18-lu-me-en ḫu-mu-un-pad3-pad3-de3-ne

70. di4-di4-la2 inim-inim-ma ḫe2-du7 kaš ḫu-mu-un-ku7-ku7-de3-ne

71. gašam ki ku10-ku10-ga ud ĝa2-ĝa2

72. sila saĝ gi4-a sila-a ba-an-ĝa2-ĝa2

73-74.
Praise Nisaba who has brought order to ...
and fixed districts in their boundaries,
the lady whose divine powers are divine powers that have no rival!

73. us2 teš2-ba ri-a si sa2-e in ki-bi sur-sur

74. nin me-ni-da me nu-sa2-a dnisaba za3-mi2

[End Scribe School]

Quotes

eme-gi-še$_3$ gu$_2$-zu na-ab-šub-be$_2$-en

"Don't neglect the Sumerian language!"

(Letter from Inim-Inanna to Lugal-ibila c.3.3.12.3.)

..

'Ipiq-Aya The Apprentice Scribe' [Google Books] p145 of *The Scribe of the Flood Story and His Circle* Ch7 p140-166 - Frans van Koppen - The Oxford Handbook of Cuneiform Culture, ed. Karen Radner, Eleanor Robson OUP '2011 (see also free download at academia.edu; a backup of the Mugsar is there too).

IPIQ-AYA, THE APPRENTICE SCRIBE

Fragments of a set of three tablets that originally contained the whole story of *Atram-hasis* in 1245 lines are nowadays located in museum collections in London, New York, and Geneva. Each tablet ends with a colophon that gives its sequence number and the name of the composition, the number of lines it contains, the name and title of the scribe, and the date when the tablet was written. This is the work of Ipiq-Aya, the 'apprentice

Google Books

The Oxford Handbook of Cuneiform Culture
edited by Karen Radner, Eleanor Robson

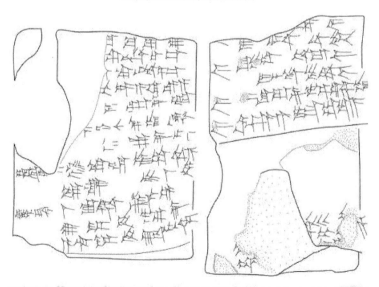

FIGURE 7.1 House rental contract: the only text written by Ipiq-Aya as a contract scribe |

Oldest Written Romance

'Ecology of Romance in Myth of Inanna' - Judy Grahn:
Inanna went into the mountains and began flying around. From one border of the territory to the other, she flew round and round. She flew around the Tree whose roots intertwine with the horizon of heaven, by now so tired that she lay down beside its boundary roots. She had in her loincloth a weaving of the seven cosmic powers, across her thighs. Her thoughts were with her shepherd lover, Dumuzid. On the same plot of land a youth, Šukaletuda, was working, and saw her; he approached, untied the loincloth of divine powers...

It was only in '1949, in an article of the volume XVII of Archive Oriental called A Blood-Plague Motif in Sumerian Mythology, that Samuel Noah Kramer translated for the first time this myth...[more: http://archive.is/wOwtq]

See also The Literature of Ancient Sumer edited Jeremy A. Black

 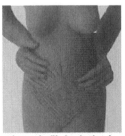

Inana's "loincloth of
7 divine powers" (Ur)

"Inanna needed to pass through the seven gates of the 'abzu' (abyss), and was not allowed to pass through unless she removed an article of clothing / jewelry for each of gate. Her clothes were symbolic of her divine power, thus she was systematically weakened in this fashion. By the time she arrived in the inner palace, she was almost naked and almost dead..."
[more: mythicjourneys.org/newsletter_oct07_prouty.html]

cf. academia.edu/1247599/Inanna_and_Sukaletuda_A_Sumerian_Astral_Myth

..

The true translation of the first written literature like Inanna's romance powers with the Mugsar 4-Way highlights that well-funded universities don't give unicodes at all, and for the sign they link off to PSD (University of Pennsylvania) where it is often not clear which is the relevant one; and their translations are superficial, probably computer generated. When you work with the actual cuneiform signs, rather than just impotent readings using our boring English phonetic script, you start to see that the scribes were not just telling a story, but literally painting the scene. When we start going deeper than such misleading translations it becomes very revealing...

Inanna and the Seven Cosmic Powers of her Loincloth

Note Intro above | 4-Way top | Very Common Signs | TOC2 112a.

u$_4$-/ba nin-ĝu$_{10}$ an\ mu-un-niĝin$_2$-na-ta

Once, lady dear heaven (flew/) roamed around,

cpd	cpd	1222C	1202D	cpd closeup
ud-ba	nin	- ĝu$_{10}$	an\	/mu-un-niĝin$_2$-na-ta\
Once 12313 UD day + 12040 BA open halve	lady, mistress 122A9 MUG cuneus + 12306 TUG$_2$ garment	'dear one' determ. / honor.	heaven	roamed around 1222C MU name + 12326 UN (KALAM = Sumer) + 121B8 niĝin$_2$ encircle + 1223E NA incense + 122EB TA much

112b.
ki /mu-un- niĝin$_2$ \-[na]-/ta\
cosmic world roamed around

121A0	cpd
⬦	𒈬𒌦𒐽𒈾𒋫
ki	/mu-un-niĝin$_2$-na-ta\
cosmic world	to roam around op. cit. 112a

113a. [Inanna top]
^{d}Inanna an mu-un-niĝin$_2$-na-ta
Inanna heaven roamed around,

12239	1202D	cpd
𒀭𒈹	𒀭	(cuneiform)
^{d}Inanna	an	/mu-un-niĝin$_2$-na-ta\
Inanna Determ. 1202D AN + 12239 MUŠ$_3$	heaven	roamed around op. cit. 112a

..

113b.
ki /mu-un- niĝin$_2$ \-[na]-/ta\
cosmos roamed around

121A0	cpd
(cuneiform)	(cuneiform)
ki	/mu-un-niĝin$_2$-na-ta\
cosmic	roamed around op. cit. 112a

114. [Inanna top]
/elam^{ki}\ su-bir$_4$^{ki}-a mu-un-niĝin$_2$-na-ta
Elam & Subir roamed around

cpd	cpd	cpd
/elam^{ki}\	su-bir$_4$^{ki}-a	/mu-un-niĝin$_2$-na-ta\
Elam	Subir	roamed around
'NIM'	122E2 SU	op. cit. 112a
1224F	skin games +	
'ki' Detern.	bir$_4$ =	
place	EDEN	
	12094 + 'ki'	
	Detern.	
	place +	
	12000 A	
	water / river	

..

115. [Inanna top]
/dubur an\ gil-gi$_{16}$-il-la mu-un-niĝin$_2$-na-ta
{[She flew around the Tree whose roots]
horizon heaven entwined roamed around,}

12135	1202D	cpd	cpd
◈	✳	𒄑𒄑𒅍𒆷	𒈬𒌦𒌋𒈾𒋫
dubur	an	gil-gi$_{16}$-il-la	/mu-un-niĝin$_2$-na-ta\
horizon	heaven	entwined 12103 gilim /gi$_{16}$ entwined + 1214B IL = high up + 121B7 LA = bend over	roamed around op. cit. 112a

..

116. [Inanna top]

nu-gig kuš$_2$-a-ni-ta im-ma-te dur$_2$-bi-še$_3$ ba-nu$_2$

Sumerian high status woman (wore bead and was black) so tired landed rump exposed [through skimpy loincloth] lay down [beside its boundary roots.]

cpd	cpd	cpd	cpd	cpd
nu-gig	kuš$_2$-a-ni-ta	im-ma-te	dur$_2$-bi-še$_3$	ba-na$_2$
Sumerian high status woman was black 1222A wore beads 1226D + 12261 NU offspring + 121C7 U$_8$ encircle	so tired uQQ kuš$_2$ tired + 12000 A cry of woe + 1224C NI come to an end + 122EB TA much	landed 1214E IM wind + 12220 MA flow + 122FC TE approach, land [cf. 12312 UB as in kiss, suck]	rump 12089 rump + + 12049 BI open + 12365 še$_3$ string [cf. loincloth]	lay down 12040 BA split, open, rump + 1223F na$_2$ lay down

etcsl.orinst.ox...c133.116

117. [Inanna top]
šu-kal-le-tud-da zag sar-ra-/ka\-ni igi im-ma-ni-/sig10\
Šukaletuda beside lair watched / perved.
[On the same plot of land a youth, Šukaletuda, was working, and saw her;]

cpd	12360	cpd	12146	cpd
𒐰𒐰𒐰𒐰𒐰	𒐰𒐰	𒐰𒐰𒐰𒐰	𒐰	𒐰𒐰𒐰𒐰
šu-kal-le-tud-da	zag	sar-ra-ka-ni	igi	im-ma-ni-sig$_{10}$
Šukaletuda	(be-)	lair	eye,	to cast
122D7 ŠU hand +	side	122AC SAR	watch	(an eye) perve
12197 KAL		garden + 1228F		1214E IM mud,
mighty + 121F7		RA thresh +		storm + 12220 MA
LE branch + 12305		12157 KA mouth		approach + 1224C
TU small, priest +		+ 1224C NI		NI finish + 122E7
12055 DA line		digest		cast

etcsl.orinst.ox...c133.117

118. [Inanna top]
^{d}Inanna-ke4 tug$_2$dara$_4$ me imin gal$_4$-la na
Inanna on reed mat [lying on her side – exposing rear view] …
loincloth divine powers seven over her cuneus/rump...
[She had in her loincloth a weaving of the seven cosmic powers,
over her cuneus/rump.]

12239+121A4	cpd	12228	12153	cpd
^{d}Inanna-ke$_4$	^{tug}dara$_4$	me	imin	gal$_4$-la-na
Inanna (DN)	loincloth	divine	seven	cuneus
Determ. 1202D	Determ.	powers	(IA 5 +	122A9 gal$_4$ cuneus
AN + 12239	12306 ^{tug}$_2$	(enabling	MIN 2)	+ 121B7 LA
MUŠ$_3$	garment +	cosmic		bending over –
+ 121A4 reed	12071	activity)		rear view cuneus
mat [lying on]	dara4 = red,			and rump in same
	brown,			angle + 1223E NA
	blood			man, pestle,
				pounder

etcsl.orinst.ox...c133.118
119. {do. 118} tug2dara4? me 7 gal4-la-na […]

Inanna & Dumuzi

120. Inanna ^dInanna ki-aĝ₂ sipad dumuzi

Inanna's thoughts were with her shpeherd lover Dumuzi

12239	cpd	cpd	cpd
^dInanna	ki-aĝ₂	sipad	lu₂-^ddumu zi-da
Inanna	loves	shepherd	dumuzi
determ. 1202D AN + 12239 MUŠ₃	121A0 KI cosmic world + 12258 aĝ₂ heat of passionate love	1227A PA overseer + 121FB UDU sheep	121FD lu₂ ruler + determ. 1202D AN 12309 + DUMU son + 12363 ZI faithful, true + 12055 DA line (gen.)

121.
gal4-la kug-ga-na lu$_2$ SU X [...]
cuneus so pure guy skin games (in the offing)

122A9+121B7	cpd	121FD	122E2
gal$_4$-la	kug-ga-na	lu$_2$	SU
cuneus op. cit. 118	(so) pure 121AC KUG pure + 120B5 suckling, carry + 1223E NA man, pestle, pounder	guy (in cool spaceship)	skin games

122.
šu-kal-le-tud-da mu-un-du₈-du₈ da-/ga\-[na ba-nu2]

Šukaletuda (Inanna about to be) 'ravaged in Sumer' [epic connotation] as in lair lay.
[std tr: Šukaletuda approached, untied the loincloth of divine powers...]

cpd	cpd	cpd	cpd
šu-kal-le-tud-da	mu-un-du₈-du₈	da-ga-na	ba-nu₂
Šukaletuda op. cit. 117	'ravaged in Sumer' 1222C name, phallus + 12326 (KALAM = Sumer) + 120EE (/12083) du₈ (GABA) x2 strip off; spread; breast; equal [*NB double emphasis on strip / ravage*]	lair 12055 DA lair + 120B5 GA suckling, hold + 1223E NA man, pestle, pounder*	lay op. cit. 116

etcsl.orinst.ox...c133.122

*Note repeated use of ⟨cuneiform⟩ GA-NA (procreation

connotation) first with ⟨cuneiform⟩ KUG (121) pure, now contrasted with

⟨cuneiform⟩ DA lair (122)

123.
ĝiš3 im-ma-ni-in-dug4 ne im-ma-[ni-in-su-ub]
skin games...

12351	cpd	12248	cpd
ĝiš₃	im-ma-ni-in-dug₄	ne	im-ma-ni-in-su-ub
phallus	mating 1214E IM storm + 12220 MA flow, come, emit* + 1224C NI orgasmic, quiver + 12154 IN abuse, rape + 12157 dug4 perform, mating	on fire	kissing... 1214E IM storm + 12220 MA flow, emit + 1224C NI orgasmic, quiver + 122E2 SU submerge, flesh, to be inside + 12312 UB praise, ruin

etcsl.orinst.ox...c133.123
Note repetition of im-ma-ni-in - probing then oral. *cf dub₃-nir

As a temple harlot one of Shamhat's several duties would be to have relations in the temple with paying 'Johns' or 'Customers', said funds being 'donated/ to the temple's upkeep. Below, a drawing after a lead votive offering found in a temple showing a 'John' having relations with a priestess atop an altar with a special incline to accomodate the act. Inanna / Ishtar [Eash-tar => Easter fertility goddess] fulfilled many roles, she was the 'Courtesan of Heaven' ('polite' scholarly language for a prostitute) and wives beseeched her aid in becoming pregnant.

"... figurines depicting relations, the man stands and the woman always rests upon a high structure, usually interpreted as an altar. These figurines may very likely represent ritual relations...they are probably in some way associated with the cult of Inanna / Ishtar as goddess of physical love and prostitution, and were, in fact found in her temple at Asshur..." [Black & Green]

... Adam and Eve in the Garden in Eden [a straight lifting from the Sumerians see 12094 – the original too cool sounding to use an inferior replacement name] being a later recasting of Enkidu and Shamhat ... thus nothing more than a recasting and sanitizing of an earlier 'ribald' Sumerian story about 'Whores and their Johns'

For more see Walter Reinhold Warttig Mattfeld on plagiarism of Enkidu and the Temple Courtesan Shamhat from the Epic of Gilgamesh for much later Adam and Eve editing; and p. 152. 'Prostitution and Ritual Sex' Jeremy Black and Anthony Green. Gods, Demons and Symbols of Ancient Mesopotamia, An Illustrated Dictionary. Austin, Texas. University of Texas Press with British Museum Press. London. '1992. And the money side see 122BA shekel.

Note other sensual compounds from PSD:

ĝeš$_3$-dug$_4$ = mating [12351 phallus + 12157 perform]

ĝeš$_3$-du$_3$ = mating [12351 phallus + 12195 perform]

na-an-du$_3$ = erect [1223E NA stone pestle + cpd {12009 a$_2$ horn + 1202D an determ. god!} a$_2$-an spadix (plant spike); erect) + 12195 perform]

124.
ĝiš3 ba-ni-in-dug₄-/ga\ [ne ba-ni-in-su-ub-ba]
skin games...
(but with more violent threshing about)

12351	cpd	12248	cpd
ĝiš₃	ba-ni-in-dug₄-ga	ne	ba-ni-in-su-ub-ba
phallus	mating* 12040 BA thresh about in mating + 1224C NI orgasmic, quiver + 12154 IN = abuse, rape + 12157 dug4 / KA = perform, mating + 120B5 GA suckling, hold	on fire	kissing...* 12040 BA thresh about in mating + 1224C NI orgasmic, quiver + 12154 IN = abuse, rape + 122E2 SU submerge, flesh, to be inside + 12312 UB praise, ruin

etcsl.orinst.ox...c133.124

*Note now the scribe replaces IM-MA with the more violent threshing about connoted by BA (but of course Inanna is so tired, she sleeps through it all, or maybe Šukaletuda was a yawn!)

125.
zag sar-ra-ka-ni im-ma-ši-/in\-[gi4]
near lair returned leering eye .

12360	cpd	cpd
zag	sar-ra-ka-ni	im-ma-ši-in-gi$_4$
near	lair	return leering eye
	122AC SAR garden	1214E IM mud, storm +
	+ 1228F RA thresh	12220 MA approach + 12146
	+ 12157 KA mouth	IGI watch + 12154 IN =
	+ 1224C NI digest	abuse + 12104 gi$_4$ return

etcsl.orinst.ox...c133.125

126.
ud im-zal ᵈutu im-ta-/e₃-a\-[ra]
day had broken and Utu had risen,

12313	1214E+1224C		12313	cpd
ud	im-zal		utu	im-ta-e₃-a-ra
day	come to pass IM mood + ZAL pass		sun (deity)	sunrise 1214E IM mood + 122EB TA much + cpd UD-DU sunrise + 12000 A bemoan + 1228F RA beat thresh

etcsl.orinst.ox...c133.126

127.
munus-e ni$_2$-te-a-ni igi im-kar$_2$-/kar$_2$\
My cuneus! checked herself anger shock

122A9	cpd	12146	1214E-uQQ
munus-e	ni$_2$-te-a-ni	igi	im-kar$_2$-kar$_2$
My cuneus! 122A9 MUNUS cuneus + 1208A E interjection - fear	fingered herself 1214E IM anger + 122FC TE cheek; penetrate; membrane + 12000 A cry of woe + 1224C NI quiver	eye	anger-shock

128.

kug ^{d}Inanna-ke$_4$ ni$_2$-te-a-ni igi im-kar$_2$-kar$_2$

purest Inanna...

121AC	12239	[do. 127]
kug	^{d}Inanna-ke$_4$	
purest	Inanna (DN)	

..

129.

ud-ba munus-e nam gal$_4$-la-na-še$_3$ a-na im-gu-lu-u$_8$-a-bi
[Then the woman was considering what should be
destroyed because of her cuneus]
Later. My cuneus! destiny – (considers) cuneus loincloth -
as much as (it takes) stirred up (for revenge)

cpd	122A9	12246	cpd	cpd	cpd
ud-ba	munus-e	nam	gal$_4$-la-na-še$_3$	a-na	im-gu-lu-u$_8$-a-bi
day 12313 UD day + 12040 BA open halve noon? Later?	My cuneus! op. cit.	destiny	cuneus loincloth 122A9 gal$_4$ cuneus + 121B7 LA + 1223E NA man, pestle, pounder + 12365 še$_3$ G-string	as much as (it takes) 12000 A + suffix element 1223E NA	stirred up (for revenge) 1214E IM anger + 12116 GU rump + 121FB LU stirred up + 121C7 U$_8$ Oh! + 12000 A bemoan + 12049 BI open [cf. 12122 GUL destroy]

etcsl.orinst.ox...c133.129

130.

kug ᵈInanna-ke₄ nam gal₄-la-na-še₃ a-na im-ak-a-bi
[Inanna was considering what should be done because of her state]
Purest Inanna – destiny – (considers) cuneus loincloth – what to do (to get revenge)

121AC	12239	12246	cpd	cpd	cpd
kug	ᵈInanna-ke₄	nam	gal₄-la-na-še₃	a-na	im-ak-a-bi
purest	Inanna (	destiny	cuneus loincloth op. cit 129	as much as (it takes) oc129	to do (revenge) 1214E IM anger + 1201D AK to do + 12000 A bemoan + 12049 BI open

etcsl.orinst.ox...c133.130

131.

pu₂ kalam-ma-ka uš₂ bi₂-ib-si-si
[She filled the wells of the Land with blood]
water wells it was said in the land of Sumer blood filled

121E5	12326	12357	122DB
pu₂	kalam-ma-ka	uš₂	bi₂-ib-si-si
water wells pu₂	it was said in the land (of Sumer) UN-MA-KA kalam 12326 UN (KALAM = Sumer) + 12220 MA land + 12157 KA talk	blood	filled 12248 bi₂ carry + 12141 IB oval + 122DB x2 SI fill (over and over)

etcsl.orinst.ox...c133.131

132.

pu$_2$-^{giš}kiri$_6$ kalam-ma-ka uš$_2$-am$_3$ i$_3$-tum$_3$-tum$_3$
[so it was blood that the irrigated orchards of the Land yielded,]
orchards it was said in the land of Sumer blood wrought havoc

122AC	12326	12357	12250
pu$_2$-^{giš}kiri$_6$	kalam-ma-ka	uš$_2$-am$_3$	i$_3$-tum$_3$-tum$_3$
orchard GIŠ-SAR 12111 ^{giš} determ. wood + kiri$_6$ orchard	it was said in the land (of Sumer) op. cit. 131	blood was 12357 uš$_2$ blood + cpd am$_3$ copula	bring (wrought havoc) 1224C i3 end up + 12250 tum$_3$ x2

etcsl.orinst.ox...c133.132

133.

arad$_2$ lu$_2$-/u$_3$ \ u$_2$ il$_2$-i-de$_3$ ĝen-na uš$_2$-am$_3$ i$_3$-na$_8$-na$_8$
[it was blood that the slave who went to collect firewood drank,]
slaves and others collecting food and firewood go blood come to drink

12035	cpd	12311	cpd	cpd	12357	12158
arad$_2$	lu$_2$-u$_3$	u$_2$	il$_2$-i-de$_3$	ĝen-na	uš$_2$-am$_3$	i$_3$-naĝ-naĝ
slaves	and others	food	collect firewood (carry) IL$_2$-I-NE 1214D il$_2$ carry + 1213F I "5" + 12248 de$_3$ collect; fire	go 1207A ĝen go + 1223E pestle	blood was op. cit 132	drink 1224C (i$_3$) come to pass + 12158 naĝ x2 drink

etcsl.orinst.ox...c133.133

134.

geme$_2$ lu$_2$-u$_3$ a si-si-de$_3$ ĝen-na uš$_2$-/am$_3$ \ [im]-mi-ib$_2$-si-si
[it was blood that the slavegirl who went out to draw water drew,]
slave girl and others water fill and carry go blood draw (from well)

cpd	cpd	12000	cpd	cpd	12357	cpd closeup
geme$_2$	lu$_2$-u$_3$	a	si-si-de$_3$	ĝen-na	uš$_2$-am$_3$	im-mi-ib$_2$-si-si
slave girl	and others	water	fill and carry 122DB SI x2 fill + 12248 de$_3$ carry	go op. cit. 133	blood was op. cit 132	draw from well 1214E IM storm, anger + 1222A MI black + 12308 ib2 cross-beam (of well) + 122DB SI x2 fill

etcsl.orinst.ox...c133.134

135.

saĝ gig₂ uš₂-/am₃ \ i₃-naĝ-naĝ zag-bi nu-/un\-zu
[and it was blood that the **black-headed people** drank.
No one knew when this would end.]
black people blood was drunk no bounds no one new

12295	1222A	12357	12158	cpd	1236A
saĝ	gig₂	uš₂-am₃	i₃-naĝ-naĝ	zag-bi	nu-un-zu
head / people	black	blood was op. cit 132	drink op. cit. 133	boundary open - endless 12360 ZAG boundary + 12049 BI open	no one knew 12261 NU not + 12326 UN one + 1236A ZU know

etcsl.orinst.ox...c133.135

136.

lu₂ ĝiš₃ dug₄-ga-ĝu₁₀ kur-kur-ra ga-mu-[ni]-/pad₃ \ im-me
[She said: "I will search the lands for the man who abused me."]
man phallus mating for years mountains find (for revenge) in the end and do battle

121FD	12351	cpd	cpd	cpd	1214E-1201E
lu₂	ĝiš₃	dug₄-ga-ĝu₁₀	kur-kur-ra	ga-mu-ni-pad₃	im-me
man	phallus	mating 12157 dug4 / KA = perform, mating + 120B5 suckling, carry + 1222C ĝu₁₀ (MU) for years	lands 121B3 KUR lands + 1228F RA aux.	find (for revenge) 120B5 GA carry + 1222C MU phallus, dear, name, son, year + 1224C NI in the end + cpd pad₃ find	battle 1214E IM wind, storm, anger / mood, to be (copula) + 1201E me₃ battle

etcsl.orinst.ox...c133.136

137.

lu₂ ĝiš₃ / dug₄\-ga-ni kur-kur-ra nu-um-/ma\-[ni-in-pad₃]-/de₃ \
[But nowhere in all the lands could she find the man who abused her.]
man phallus mating time passes in all the lands could not find rapist

121FD	12351	cpd	cpd	cpd
(sign)	(sign)	(sign)	(sign)	(sign)
lu₂	ĝiš₃	dug₄-ga-ni	kur-kur-ra	nu-um-ma-ni-in-pad₃-de₃
man	phallus	mating	lands	in all the lands
		12157 dug4	121B3	could not find rapist
		perform,	KUR	12261 NU not +
		mating +	lands	1231D UM approach, disease
		120B5 GA	+	+ 12220 MA land; approach
		suckling,	1228F RA	+ 1224C NI in time
		carry +	[phrase	+ 12154 IN rapist
		1224C NI	ender]	+ cpd pad₃ find
		time passes		+ 12248 de₃ carry

etcsl.orinst.ox...c133.137

138a.

[i₃-ne-eš₂ lu₂-u₃] / lu₂\-ra a-na na-an-dug₄
[Now, what did one say to another?]
time passes this Inanna loincloth this man and others what mating with the gods

cpd	cpd	121FD	cpd	
i₃-ne-eš₂	lu₂-u₃	lu₂-ra	a-na	na-an-dug₄
(now - Akk *Inanna*) 1224C i₃ time passes + 12248 NE fire; this + 12365 eš₂ string (loincloth)	man and 121FD lu₂ man / him + 12147 u₃ and	others 121FD lu₂ man + 1228F RA aux.	what 12000 A wonder + 1223E NA aux.]	mating with the gods 1223E NA stone, pestle + 1202D AN gods + 12157 dug4 perform, mating

etcsl.orinst.ox...c133.138

138b.

/ lu₂-u₃ \ [lu₂-ra dili a-na na-an-taḫ]
[What further did one add to the other in detail?]
man and other one what add for the gods (why should they live)

cpd	121FD	12038	cpd	cpd
lu₂-u₃	lu₂-ra	dili	a-na	na-an-taḫ
man and 121FD lu₂ man / him + 12147 u₃ and	other 121FD lu₂ man + 1228F RA aux.	ones	what 12000 A wonder + 1223E NA aux.]	add for the gods 1223E NA stone, pestle + 1202D AN gods + 1222D taḫ add

etcsl.orinst.ox...c133.138

[Continues: Black Sumerian city-dwellers – father's advises
Šukaletuda to join brothers]

The song of lettuce, t.4.08.05 (etcsl.orinst.ox.ac.uk/cgi-bin/etcsl.cgi?text=t.4.08.05)

Vigorously he sprouted, vigorously he sprouted and sprouted, water it - it being
lettuce!
In his black garden of the desert bearing much yield did my darling of his mother,
My barley stalk full of allure in its furrow, water it - it being lettuce,
Did my one - a very apple tree bearing fruit at the top – water it - it being a garden!
The honey-sweet man, the honey-sweet man, was doing sweet (things) to me!
My lord, the honey-sweet man, the godly one, my darling of his mother,
His hands honey sweet, his feet honeying, was doing sweet (things) to me!
His limbs being sweet his feet honeying, was doing sweet (things) to me!
His limbs being sweet, sweet honey, he was doing sweet things to me!

O my one who of a sudden was doing sweet (things) to the
whole (insides up) to the navel, my darling of his mother,
My desert-honey loins, darling of his mother, you watered it - it being lettuce!

The lettuce, mentioned in these texts (hi-iz^{sar} [1212D]) is probably *Lactuta sativa*...
In Sumerian texts it is generally associated with cuneus.. Jacobson thought it
represented the pubic hair. Maybe the visual aspect is less important here, although
the overlapping leaves and their texture, as well as milky or clear sap, are quite
evocative, lettuces and similar fast growing vegetables, like cucumbers and melons,
all of which were grown in Mesopotamian gardens, require frequent watering ...
association with water might also have contributed to the metaphorical range: the
cuneus, like lettuce, is said to need the 'watering' ...

We have seen that làl ('honey') is frequently used to describe sensual pleasure. The
expression 'to taste the honey-plant' was a common euphemism for relations. Here
the lover is equated with the sensation he brings - his very limbs are 'honey', they
'bring sweetness', orgasmic enjoyment. The metaphor extends from activity ('to do
the sweet thing [same sign 1212D HI]') and personal attributes ('whose limbs are
honey') to the location... This 'honey' was date-syrup rather than the bees' product.

..

A balbale to Inanna, t.4.08.4 (etcsl.orinst.ox.ac.uk/cgi-bin/etcsl.cgi?text=t.4.08.04)
alternative translation Alster 1993:

The brother makes me enter his house:
He made me lie on a honey-smelling bed,
After my precious, dear one, had lain by my heard,
One-by-one, making "tongues", one by one,
My brother of the fairest face made fifty.
He became (?) like a silenced man
With an 'earthquake' he was put to silence.
My brother, with a hand put on his waist,
My precious, sweet one, the time passes!
(Lover:) Se me free, my sister, set me free!

Come, my beloved sister, let us go to the palace (var. to our house)!
May you be a little daughter in my father's eyes!"

Leick gives the Sumerian of one of the lines in part because of its 'delightful resonances':

dili-dili-ta eme-ak dili-dili-ta
One by one - making tongues - one by one

'eme-ak' (tongue making) usually implies speaking, chatting (the proverbial 'sweet nothings'?). But it could also have, as Alster duly noted, a double meaning, and imply lovemaking. The following lines speak in favor of a sensual meaning, as the 'brother' is silenced by an 'earthquake' - surely a reference to an orgasm - although Inanna is willing to continue this form of passing time. Again the scenario is one of pre-martial love making, with the man expressing his desire to formulate their union, since the last line explicitly says that a girl should become a daughter-in-law to his father. The text is imbued with a sense of irony, that the inexperienced ki-sikil is well able to exhaust the ardour of her lover, even rather overtaking his virility."

cf. *Oath of Women* (A balbale to Inanna Dumuzid B) t.4.08.02
(etcsl.orinst.ox.ac.uk/cgi-bin/etcsl.cgi?text=t.4.08.02&display=Crit&charenc=&lineid=t40802.p1#t40802.p1)

My juicy, grape, my honey sweet...
May you put your right hand in my cuneus,
With your left stroke my head,
When you have brought your mouth close to my mouth,
When you have taken my lips in your mouth,
By so doing you wil swear an oath to me...

etcsl.orinst.oxc40802.21

21-26. You are to place your right hand on my cuneus
while your left hand rests on my head,
bringing your mouth close to my mouth,
and taking my lips in your mouth:
thus you shall take an oath for me.
This is the oath of women

[Mesopotamian Literature, Gwendolyn Leick; etcsl.orinst.ox.c40805.1
(etcsl.orinst.ox.ac.uk/edition2/etcslgloss.php?lookup=c40805.1&charenc=gcirc&sn=ON)]

Gudea Cylinders

The Gudea cylinders are a pair of terracotta cylinders dating to circa 7875 CT [2125 *plag*] on which is written in cuneiform a Sumerian myth called the Building of Ningursu's temple.[1] The cylinders were found in '1877 during excavations at Telloh (ancient Girsu), Iraq and are now displayed in the Louvre in Paris, France. They are the largest cuneiform cylinders yet discovered and contain the longest known text written in the Sumerian language... [Wik]

The god of wisdom, Enki, organized the world after creation and gave each deity a role in the world order. *Nisaba was named the scribe of the gods*, and Enki then built her a school of learning so that she could better serve those in need.

Nidaba / Nindaba / Nisaba = goddess of writing (and teaching) she was often praised by Sumerian scribes. Many clay-tablets end with the phrase

 DINGIR.NAGA.ZAG.SAL, ^{d}nisaba za$_3$-mi$_2$, "Nisaba be praised" to honor the goddess. She is considered the teacher of both mortal scribes and other divine deities...

As the goddess of knowledge, she is related to many other facets of intellectual study and other gods may turn to her for advice or aid. Some of these traits are shared with her sister Ninsina. She is also associate with grain, reflecting her association with an earth goddess mother.

12240   NAGA = potash; soap

AN.NAGA is read as NANIBGAL, and AN.ŠE.NAGA as NÁNIBGAL. NAGA is read as NÍDABA or NÍSABA, and ŠE.NAGA as NIDABA or NISABA...[Wik]

specialtyinterests.net/cuneiform_writing.html

etcsl.orinst.ox...t.2.1.7#

SUMERIAN CUNEIFORM DICTIONARY

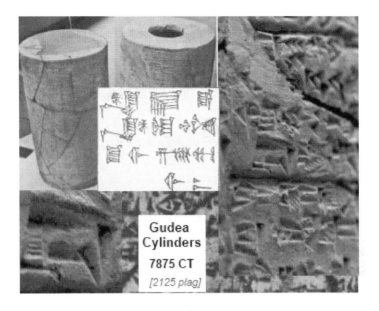

..

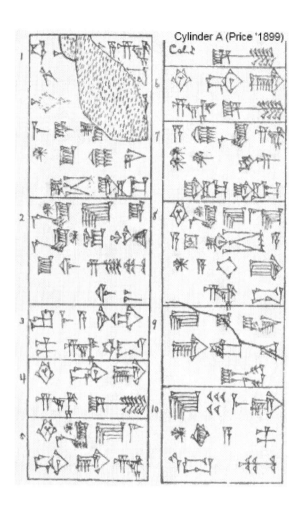

Cylinder A (Price '1899)

The Building of Ningirsu's Temple

Gudea Cylinders A and B (c.2.1.7), line c217.110
Paragraph t217.p14 (line(s) 110-114)

..

110. munus 1(DIŠ)-am₃ a-ba me-a nu a-ba me-a-ni
[ETCSL: Then there was a woman -- whoever she was.]
woman one was who "to be or not to be"*

122A9	cpd	cpd	12228	12261	cpd	12228
munus	DIŠ-am₃	a-ba	me	nu	a-ba	me
woman	one was	who	to be	not	who	to be
	12079	12000 A			12000 A	
	DIŠ one	progeny			progeny	
	+ cpd	+ 12040			+ 12040	
	A-AN	BA			BA	
	copula	share			share	

*So that's where Shakespeare / Edward de Vere plagiarized it from!
http://cdli.ox.ac.uk/etcsl/...c217.110

111. saĝ-ĝa₂ e₃ ki garadin₉ mu-ak
[ETCSL: She ...... sheaves.]
head basket bring place sheaves do

cpd	cpd	121A0	1230F	cpd
saĝ-ĝa₂	e₃	ki	garadin₉	mu-ak
head basket	bring	place	sheaf	to do
12295 saĝ	12313 UD		/ bundle	1222C MU
head	sun +		(of reeds)	name
+ 120B7	1207A			+ 1201D AK do
ĝa2 basket	DU leave,			
	bring			

112. gi-dub-ba kug NE-a šu im-mi-du$_8$
[ETCSL: She held a stylus of refined silver in her hand,]
stylus silver refined hand proudly displayed

cpd	121AC	cpd	122D7	cpd
gi-dub-ba	kug	NE-A	šu	im-mi-du$_8$
(reed tablet) stylus 12100 GI reed stem + 1207E DUB tablet + 12040 BA divide tool	silver, shiny metal	refined 12248 NE brazier + 12000 A water	hand	(proudly) display 1214E IM mood, is (copula) + 1222A MI black [cf miqtum (high) class?] + 120EE (/12083) du$_8$ (GABA); spread

http://cdli.ox...c217.112

113. dub mul-an dug$_3$-ga im-mi-ĝal$_2$
[ETCSL: and placed it on a tablet with propitious stars,]
tablet cosmic star good ones classified

1207E	cpd	cpd	cpd
dub	mul-an	dug$_3$-ga	im-mi-ĝal$_2$
tablet	cosmic star 1202F MUL star + 1202D AN cosmic	good ones 1212D dug3 good + 120B5 GA suckling, carry	classified 1214E IM mood, (copula) + 1222A MI black, high ?? + 12145 ĝal$_2$ place class ?? cf. mi-iq-tum (miqtum, mi-ĝal$_2$-tum) social class

..
114. ad im-dab$_6$-gi$_4$-gi$_4$
[ECSL: and was consulting it."]
recited (mantra) turning round and round

1201C	cpd
ad	im-dab$_6$-gi$_4$-gi$_4$
voice, cry, recited (mantra) ??	turning round and round 1214E IM mood, (copula) 1234F dab$_6$ go around, + 12104 gi$_4$ x2 turn, go around [gi$_4$ x 2 therefore: 'turn round and round' ??]

..

ETCSL:

"Then there was a woman -- whoever she was.
She ...... sheaves [bundles].
She held a stylus of refined silver in her hand,
and placed it on a tablet with propitious stars,
and was consulting it."

..

110. munus 1(DIŠ)-am$_3$ a-ba me-a nu a-ba me-a-ni
111. saĝ-ĝa$_2$ e$_3$ ki garadin$_9$ mu-ak
112. gi-dub-ba kug NE-a šu im-mi-du$_8$
113. dub mul-an dug$_3$-ga im-mi-ĝal$_2$
114. ad im-dab$_6$-gi$_4$-gi$_4$

Very Common Signs

1228F	1224C	1231D	1222C	12326	120B5
RA	NI	UM	MU	UN	GA
1228F RA (rah$_2$) kill; flood; aux.	1224C NI (i$_3$) comes to pass; quiver	1231D UM approach, disease	1222C MU (ĝu$_{10}$) year, dear, name, son, phallus 43667x!	12326 UN people (KALAM / Sumer)	120B5 GA suckling, carry, bring

..

12157	12261	12154	1214E	12220	12248
dug4	NU	IN	IM	MA	NE
12157 dug4 perform, mating	12261 NU not	12154 IN abuse	1214E IM wind, storm, anger / mood, is (copula)	12220 MA land; approach	12248 NE fire; this

..

1222A	122E1	1202D	cpd	121FD	121A0	12000
gig₂	SILA₃	AN	nin	lu₂	ki	A
1222A gig₂ / MI black	122E1 SILA₃ vessel, capacity 43696x!	heaven	lady, mistress 122A9 cuneus + 12306 garment	man	cosmic world; place 32379x!	water / river; bemoan; progeny

cpd	12309	12365	1208D	1207E	cpd
pad₃	dumu	eš₂	e₂	DUB	dub-sar
find, discover; name, nominate 12146 IGI eye + 12292 RU fall; throw	child, son, daughter; apprentice 28245x! TUR = small	flour, rope, string	house, school, temple	tablet, document	scribe 1207E DUB tablet + 122AC SAR write

SUMERIAN CUNEIFORM DICTIONARY

12313	12040	cpd	120FB	1207A	12195
UD	BA	ud-ba	GAR	DU	DU
day, once...	divide, allot, share; open; halve; noun-aux.	Once... Later... noon 12313 UD day + 12040 BA open halve	bread; ĝar place; niĝ₂ thing	(gen) go, come	build, perform

..

122A9	1223E	cpd			
MUG	NA	kur-kur-ra			
SAL, munus woman, matriarch, queen, goddess, cuneus	1223E NA incense, (burner) pestle	lands 121B3 KUR lands + 1228F RA aux.			

..

Not Translated Tablet (Gudean Period)

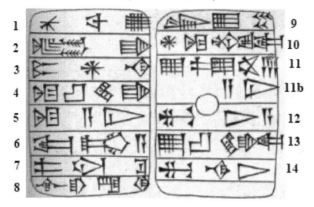

Mmnm ... not translated huh? Let's apply **Mugsar 4-Way** and see how far we get...

Line **1**

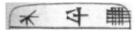

..

	12040	12311
	BA	U$_2$
	allot	food

..

Line 2

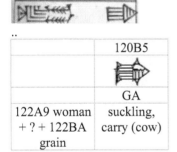

..

	120B5
	GA
122A9 woman + ? + 122BA grain	suckling, carry (cow)

Line 3

..

12309		1202D	1223E
dumu		AN	NA
child, son, daughter; apprentice		heaven	incense; pestle

..

Line 4

..

cpd		121AC	120B5
NIN		KUG	GA
lady, mistress 122A9 cuneus + 12306 garment	cf. 12085 SHEKEL grain price	KU₃, kug pure	GA suckling, carry (cow)

Line 5

..

cpd	12000	1224C
NIN	A	NI
lady, mistress 122A9 cuneus + 12306 garment	water / river; bemoan	(i₃) in time; quiver

..

Line 6

..

	12323	12000
	SIMUG	A
cf. 12295 head (var)	metal worker cf. 12324 winnow	water / river; bemoan

Line 7

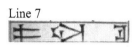

..

1227A	122EB	122DB
PA	TA	SI
overseer; branch; sceptre	much; from	fill, load; horn

..

Line 8

..

	12053	121B7	121A0
	BUR	LA	KI
	food offering; priest	rump, bend over, hang, show, supervise	cosmic world

Line 9 (right side)

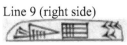

..

121FD		
🐟		𒈺
lu₂		
man		? numeric 1230D (50) | cf. 122BA 𒈺 barley

..

Line 10

..

1202D	cpd	12108		
✳	𒎙	🐟		𒐕
AN	NIN	GIR		
heaven	lady, mistress 122A9 cuneus + 12306 garment	knife, sword		cf. 12295 head (var)

Line 11

..

121A4	1227A		12153
KID	PA		IMIN
field, mat	overseer; branch; sceptre		7 (5+2)

..

Line 11b

12000	1224C
A	NI
water / river; bemoan	(i₃) in time; quiver

Line 12

..

1222C	12195	12000
MU	KAK	A
1222C MU (ĝu₁₀) phallus, dear, name, son, year	build, perform	water / river; bemoan

..

Line 13

..

121A4		121AC	120B5	12157
KID		KUG	GA	KA
field, mat		KU₃, kug pure	suckling, carry	mouth; speak; perform

Line 14

..

1222C	1223E	12195
MU	NA	KAK
($\hat{g}u_{10}$) phallus, dear, name, son, year	incense; pestle	build, perform

..

cf. etcsl.orinst.ox...c432e.D.54

A šir-namšub to Utu (Utu E) (c.4.32.e), line c432e.D.54

lu$_2$	zid-zid-da-ke$_4$	kaš-zu	bur-ra	me-ri	ki	a-da-ab-KU
LU$_2$	ZI-ZI-DA-KID	BI-ZU	BUR-RA	ME-RI	KI	A-DA-AB-KU
lu$_2$	zid	kaš	bur	ğiri$_3$ (ES: me-ri)	ki	KU
person	right	beer	type of bowl	foot	place	KU

Paragraph t432e.p10 (line(s) 51-58)

51. mu-lu zid-de$_3$ mu-lu zid-zid-da-[ke$_4$] gu$_2$-bi mu-un-ši-ib$_2$-[gi$_4$]
52. u$_3$-mu-un erim$_6$-ma kur gal ^{d}mu-ul-lil$_2$ gu$_2$-bi mu-un-ši-ib$_2$-gi$_4$
53. **nin** erim$_6$-ma ama gal ^{d}**nin**-lil$_2$ gu$_2$-bi mu-un-ši-[ib$_2$-gi$_4$]
54. lu$_2$ zid-zid-da-ke$_4$ kaš-zu bur-ra me-ri ki a-da-ab-KU
55. zabar-bi ši su$_3$-ud-ma-al de$_3$-ra-ab-dirig-ge
56. nibru^{ki} du$_3$-du$_3$-a-ba X KI X X X-a-ba še-eb e$_2$-e X-a-ba
57. dam til$_3$-la e$_2$ X [...] dirig$^?$-ge
58. a e$_2$-a a X [...]

51. The righteous man, the most righteous of men, has filled them to overflowing.
52. O lord of the storehouse, Great Mountain Enlil, he has filled them to overflowing.
53. O **lady** of the storehouse, great mother Ninlil, he has filled them to overflowing.
54. The most righteous of men has ...... the **bowls** with your beer.
55. May this bronze vessel increase his long life.
56. When Nibru had been fully built, when ...... had been ......, when the brickwork of this house had been ......,
57. the living spouse ......,
58. the seed of the house, the seed ....

cf. Line 8

..

	12053		121A0
	BUR		KI
	food offering; priest		cosmic world

SUMERIAN CUNEIFORM DICTIONARY

REFERENCE & LINKS

PSD

psd.museum.upenn.edu/epsd1/nepsd-frame.html - Pennsylvania Sumerian Dictionary Project - could have been fantastic, except that they seem to think it was perfect and stopped back in '2006 - no interest in unicodes / putting everything together.
Anyway, once you get the hang of it, you can see Steve Tinney and his colleagues have still done a terrific job.

Early Dynastic and Early Sargonic Tablets from Adab - Giuseppe Visicato, Aage Westenholz 2010; Bureaucracy of Fara - Giuseppe Visicato 1995; The Proto-Elamite Texts from Tepe Yahya 1989 – Peter Damerow, Robert K Englund, OrNS 1995; K. Maekawa, Mesopotamia 1973-74, ASJ – 1982, 1987; A. Cavigneaux and F. Alrawi 2002; P. Steinkeller SDU 1989, 1995; Earliest Land Tenure Systems in the Near East: Kudurrus. I. J. Gelb, P. Steinkeller, and R. M. Whiting, Jr. 1991; W. Sallaberger, Kalender 1993; M. Sigrist, Drehem 1992; C. Wilcke, ZA 1996; M. Stol, BSA 1995; M. Sigrist, Drehem 1992; W. Sallaberger, Ur III-Zeit 1999; F. Pomponio and G. Visicato, ED Szuruppak 1994; J.N. Postgate and P. Steinkeller, LAT 1992, SDU 1989; M. van de Mieroop, Isin crafts 1987; T. Maeda, ASJ 1982; P. Steinkeller, AuOr, SDU 1989 ; J. Hoyrup, Lengths Widths Surfaces 2002; W. Rollig and H. Waetzoldt, RlA 1993-1997; P. Attinger and M. Krebernik, Schretter 2004; M. Powell, Drinking in Ancient Societies 1994

..

ETCSL

http://etcsl.orinst.ox.ac.uk/ - The Electronic Text Corpus of Sumerian Literature (ETCSL), a project of the University of Oxford, comprises a selection of nearly 400 literary compositions [Jeremy Black ['1951-'2004, founder]

ETCSL Search

Fast Find: substitute in hypertext edit composition parameters composition c.1.3.3 line 129 = c133.129
etcsl.orinst.ox.ac.uk/edition2/etcslgloss.php?lookup=c133.129&charenc=gcirc&sn=ON

..

Sumerian Cuneiform Pioneers

As mentioned earlier the problem with fancy databases of the zillion dollar endowment elite university professors with lifetime salaries is that plebs like us (especially considering the average web user's short attention span of 5 nano seconds) struggle to find actual Sumerian cuneiform on their databases – just boring pages of English alphabet. That you now get straight up with the Mugsar QuickFinder and 4-Way. So for true reference, to really get a feel for what the Sumerian scribes were trying to say, it seems easier to go back to the Sumerian cuneiform ~~icebraking~~ codebreaking pioneers of a century ago, like these guys below where you can instantly and easily browse their works on the amazing Internet Archive:

Sumerian Tablets from Umma - Published '1915 Ed. Charles Lees Bedale ('1879-'1919) - Internet Archive

Sumerian Epics And Myths Cuneiform Series III- Published '1934 - Edward Chiera (b. Rome '1885 - d. Chicago '1933) – Internet Archive

A Sumerian Reading Book - Published '1924 - C.J. Gadd - Internet Archive

The Exaltation of Inanna - Enheduanna - William W. Hallo and J. J. A. van Dijk - Published '1968

Sumerian Proverbs - glimpses of everyday life in Mesopotamia - Edmund I. Gordon, Ed. Thorkild Jacobsen - Published '1959

Creation, Deluge ...Legends of the Gods - Cuneiform Inscriptions - Published '1876 – Internet Archive - George Smith (b. '1840 London - d. dysentery '1876 Aleppo Syria) first to discover and translate *The Epic of Gilgamesh*.

For links and updates see online Mugsar Reference:
australiansofarabia.wordpress.com/mugsar-sumerian-cuneiform-dictionary-reference-and-credits/

..

Unicode Sign closeup

scriptsource.org

..

Closeups of actual signs on tablets

John Heise Top 20 Cuneiform   12000 A =
water (shame he seems to have disappeared after '1996)

..

List of determinatives

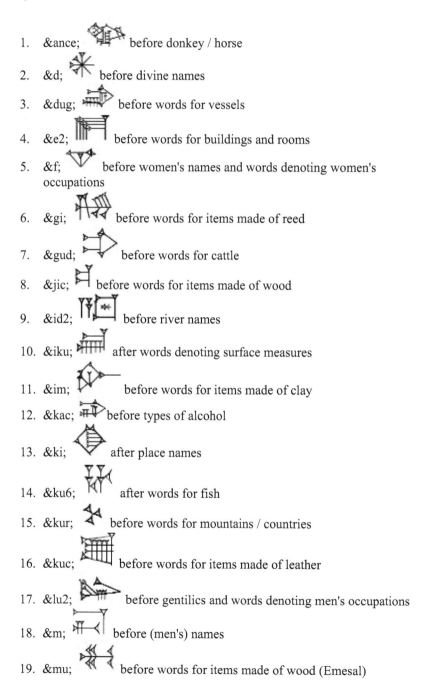

1. &ance;   before donkey / horse

2. &d;   before divine names

3. &dug;   before words for vessels

4. &e2;   before words for buildings and rooms

5. &f;   before women's names and words denoting women's occupations

6. &gi;   before words for items made of reed

7. &gud;   before words for cattle

8. &jic;   before words for items made of wood

9. &id2;   before river names

10. &iku;   after words denoting surface measures

11. &im;   before words for items made of clay

12. &kac;   before types of alcohol

13. &ki;   after place names

14. &ku6;   after words for fish

15. &kur;   before words for mountains / countries

16. &kuc;   before words for items made of leather

17. &lu2;   before gentilics and words denoting men's occupations

18. &m;   before (men's) names

19. μ   before words for items made of wood (Emesal)

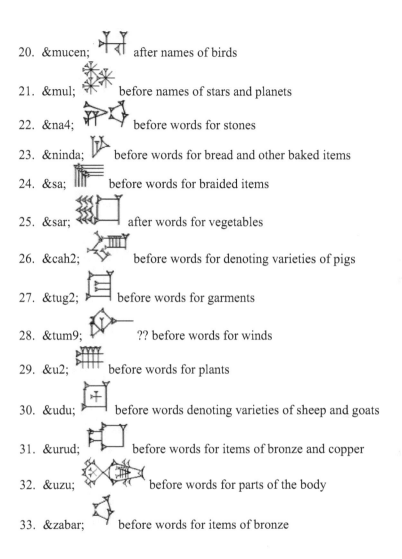

20. &mucen; after names of birds

21. &mul; before names of stars and planets

22. &na4; before words for stones

23. &ninda; before words for bread and other baked items

24. &sa; before words for braided items

25. &sar; after words for vegetables

26. &cah2; before words for denoting varieties of pigs

27. &tug2; before words for garments

28. &tum9; ?? before words for winds

29. &u2; before words for plants

30. &udu; before words denoting varieties of sheep and goats

31. &urud; before words for items of bronze and copper

32. &uzu; before words for parts of the body

33. &zabar; before words for items of bronze

..

Misc.

ORACC: oracc.museum.upenn.edu The Open Richly Annotated Cuneiform Corpus

BDTNS: bdts.filol.csic.es

Sumerian Lexicon pdf & The Proto-Sumerian Language Invention Process – John Halloran - sumerian.org

Literature of Ancient Sumer, Jeremy Black - Google Books

SUMERIAN CUNEIFORM DICTIONARY

The Initiative for Cuneiform Encoding (ICE: jhu.edu/ice)

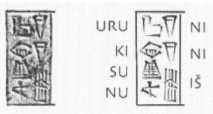

Proto Cuneiform Signs – CDLI (Oxford/UCLA)

CDLI: cdli.ucla.edu Cuneiform Digital Library Initiative – note Late
Uruk Period signs - full list of proto-cuneiform signs – pdf:
cdli.ucla.edu/tools/SignLists/ATU1.pdf - 'MUG' 122A9 examples:

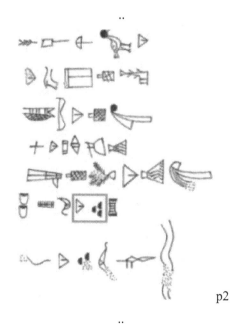

p1

p2

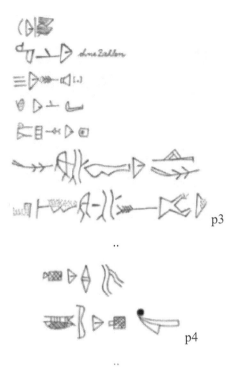

p3

p4

Late Uruk Period Cattle Dairy Products – Englund (pdf cdli)

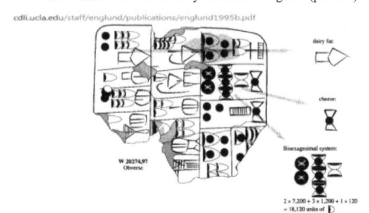

Figure 5: Simple accounts of dairy products from the Uruk IV period (above; copies from R. Englund, ATU 5) and a large account from the Uruk III period (below; see ATU 2, pl. 55, and Archaic Bookkeeping, p. 94) of products from animal husbandry, including the signs for dairy fat (DUG$_b$) and cheese (GA'AR).

LAK (proto list)

(*Liste der archaischen Keilschriftzeichen 1922* WVDOG 40, Berlin)

cdli.ucla.edu/tools/SignLists/LAK/HTML/P0001.html

(UCLA Cuneiform Digital Library Initiative)

LAK is a dictionary of Sumerian cuneiform signs of the pre-classical Fara period (Early Dynastic II), published in '1922 by Sumerologist P. Anton Deimel ('1865–'1954). The list enumerates 870 distinct cuneiform signs.

The sign inventory in the archaic period was considerably larger than the standard inventory of texts of the classical Sumerian (7400-7650CT [2600-2350plag]) or Neo-Sumerian (7900CT; all dates short chronology) periods. This means that numerous signs identified by their classical reading continue several distinct signs of the pre-classical period. If it is necessary to identify the pre-classical sign intended, its LAK number is customarily given, in the form of LAK-1 to LAK-870 [Wik].

http://www.cdli.ucla.edu/tools/SignLists/LAK/HTML/P0001.html

1	▷— . Zahleinheit junges Fischchen	R, PW, 9070, 8; 12729, 14; ^dR-nab, 12806, 1/3. R^{ba}, 12751, 1; ^dR-nab-ĝb/gud/amar/an, 12180; R^{Gu}, 9124, 8; R-nab-ab, 12523,4. R-mun^{bu} 9124,8; R-nab-mu, 9124,3; s. 9112,5; R-sahar^{ku}, 9124,9. s. die Zahlzeichen; lú + R. Zuweilen $R = 5$, z. B. ^{gis}R-uš$^{} = ^{gis}$bar-uš, 12625,11; 11729; s. auch zabar. iš-R(= num)-mu SAK 22, 5, 12.	▷─ ; Y
2	◁	R^{ba} (Var. von 3), 12251, 1; 12695,2; s. ▷— ^{ba}; s. die Zahlz. du-R-da, 12574, 10.	
	◁, —	s. die Zahlz.	
3	▷▷►	R^{ba} (Var. von 2), 12693,2; 12751,1.	
	▷◁─, ▷❯◁	s. n. 46.	
4	◁▷ , ▷◁ s. Zahlz. (=14 gan) und ?	^dR, 12760, 13; R_{ub}-ud-ub, 12503,1; R·····ku, 12503,4 gan·$R\begin{vmatrix} ^d \\ gan·R \end{vmatrix} ^{šú}ki$, 9124,2; R-nun-ud $^d Ur$, 12582,3. igi-R-kur ▨▨▨ , 9112,9; R-kur ◆▶ 12606,3 R-kur ▷◯ , 12680,7. nun-tüg-ru	
5	✳ s. etwas Geteiltes	^dR, 12737,4; R-la, s. Frauennam. bei Urukag. R-dur-a, 12778,2; gal-R-dur, 9130,6. RTC 58 Zf. in allen arch. T. R(= kalag?)-ha-šam, BP 222;	▷—
6	◈ s. Lanzenspitze, Messer ?	R, pass. in allen arch. T.; $^d Nin$ ◈◈ (Var ◈, ◈). su, Déc. ép. p. XXXIV; ◯ , Blau (= Brit. Mus. n. 86260)	▷◁░
7	◈ s. lanzettförmiges (Myrten?) Blatt.	R, pass. in allen arch. T.; id R-ka-kam, Fö. 1233. 40 ma-na ^{šim}R, 73A 6,2; 10 ma-na R.; Amherst? Oft Syn. von n.6	▷◁░
8	✴ "Stern"	pass. in allen arch. T.; verziertes R: ✳ , REC 5 bis 12606, R ✽ R-na; R-ra/ri/rí, pass	▷◁

DOG. Deimel: Fara.

Civilization Time

CT	*plagio*	Event
0	*-10000*	End of the last Ice Age, allows sedentary living and the rise of civilization
6600	*-3400*	Writing invented by the black Sumerians - first students and professors, the original gods, first epic, Gilgamesh, creation and flood myths complete with ark, calendar festivals like birth and death of Marduk bull calf of sun god Utu - northern hemisphere December Solstice => Roman Saturnalia => religio plagiarists, spring equinox rebirth festival fertility goddess Innana => Ishtar => Oestre => Easter, invention of the wheel, sexagesimal (base 60) system, first law codes, first details of musical instruments, the true etymology of many Greek/Roman words, all subsequently recorded on clay tablets. Instead of being lauded as pioneers, they are now categorized as 'ancient' – supposedly everything they achieved has no connection to the plagiarists.
9956	*-45*	Sosigenes of Alexandria's Western Calendar for Julius Caesar begins
10000	*-1**	No extant record of anything significant happening, as confirmed by Dead Sea Scrolls. So why do modern, enlightened, non-racist sapiens have to start counting backwards and insult the achievements of the Sumerians (and Kumets aka Egyptians)?!
10001	*+1**	do. ** The plagiarists forgot to put in a zero year!*
10100	*+100*	China invents paper replacing brittle papyrus. Later they would add weapon superiority gun powder.

10600	+600	India invents our numeral system replacing cumbersome Roman numerals.
10340	+340	Denis Little plagiarizes Sosigenes' calendar for religio bureaucrats – by chance events, plagio-religio impostor would be forced on all cultures for international dating, even in government and law courts where constitutionally there is supposed to be separation of state and religio; beginning of Dark Ages – writing lost to all but a few, who rehash the same group of plagiarized stories, for 1000 years until the Renaissance / Enlightenment
12013	+2013	December 4th

A little bit of video of Tara (then 6 yo) making and 'unearthing' the CT Book on YouTube:

1. **Unearthing the CT Book** (16s)
youtu.be/_kmiWiLdki4
2. **Tara Designing CT Book** (1m 41s)
youtu.be/rk0Qp03Vv2Q

ISBN: 978-0-646-50793-4

CIVILIZATION TIME BOOK - BOX TEMPLATE

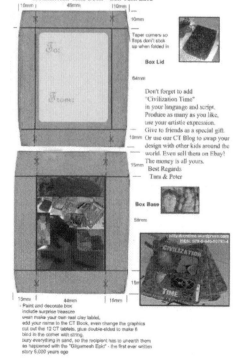

10mm | 49mm | 110mm

10mm

Taper corners so
flaps don't stick
up when folded in

Box Lid

64mm

Don't forget to add
"Civilization Time"
in your language and script.
Produce as many as you like,
use your artistic expression.
Give to friends as a special gift.
Or use our CT Blog to swap your
design with other kids around the
world. Even sell them on Ebay!
The money is all yours.
Best Regards
Tara & Peter

Box Base

58mm

15mm

15mm | 44mm | 15mm

- Paint and decorate box
include surprise treasure
even make your own real clay tablet,
add your name in the CT Book, even change the graphics
cut out the 12 CT tablets, glue double-sided to make 6
bind in the corner with string,
bury everything in sand, so the recipient has to unearth them
as happened with the "Gilgamesh Epic" - the first ever written
story 5,000 years ago

Sumer Periods

Sumer Periods [Wik]

Ubaid period (Chalcolithic)	Uruk XIV-V Uruk period (Late Chalcolithic)	Uruk IV Uruk II	Early Dynastic period I IIa IIIb Akkadian	Gutian Ur III

```
4700 4900 5100 5300 5500 5700 5900 6100 6300 6500 6700 6900 7100 7300 7500 7700 7900 CT
├─┼─┼─┼─┼─┼─┼─┼─┼─┼─┼─┼─┼─┼─┼─┼─┼─┤
-5300 -5100 -4900 -4700 -4500 -4300 -4100 -3900 -3700 -3500 -3300 -3100 -2900 -2700 -2500 -2300 -2100
```

Religio-plagiarized system

Ubaid = 5000-6000CT (5000-4000 *religio-plagio*) – Early settlements in Sumer (southern Iraq).

Uruk = 6000-7000CT (4000-3000 *plag*) – Civilization develops rapidly through cuneiform writing.

Early Dynastic = 7000-7650CT (3000-2350 *plag*) – Independent, sometimes conflicting Sumerian city states. [Literature of Ancient Sumer, Jeremy Black]

ED IIIa = The Early Dynastic IIIa (Fara) period - c.7400-7500CT (2600-2500 *plag*)

ED IIIb period = c. 7460-7650CT (2540-2350 *plag*)

The Early Dynastic period began after a cultural break with the preceding Jemdet Nasr period that has been radio-carbon dated to about [7100CT (2900 *plag*)] at the beginning of the Early Dynastic I Period. No inscriptions have yet been found verifying any names of kings that can be associated with the Early Dynastic I period. The ED I period is distinguished from the ED II period by the narrow cylinder seals of the ED I period and the broader wider ED II seals engraved with banquet scenes or animal-contest scenes. The Early Dynastic II period is when Gilgamesh, the famous king of Uruk, is believed to have reigned. Later inscriptions have been found bearing some Early Dynastic II names from the King List. The Early Dynastic IIIa period is when syllabic writing began. Accounting records and an undeciphered logographic script existed before the Fara Period, but the full flow of human speech was first recorded around [7400CT (2600*plag*)] at the beginning of the Fara Period.

Hegemony, which came to be conferred by the Nippur priesthood, alternated among a number of competing dynasties, hailing from Sumerian city-states traditionally including Kish, Uruk, Ur, Adab and Akshak, as well as some from outside of southern Mesopotamia, such as Awan, Hamazi, and Mari, until the Akkadians, under Sargon of Akkad, overtook the area...

Ur III = The Third Dynasty of Ur: 107 years, 7954-8061CT (2047–1940 *plag*)
[cf. 108 years, 7888-7996CT (2112–2004 *plag*) - Black, ibid.]

Also known as the Neo-Sumerian Empire or the Ur III Empire, refers to a Sumerian ruling dynasty based in the city of Ur and a short-lived territorial-political state that some historians regard as a nascent empire... [Wik]

The Third Dynasty of Ur came to preeminent power in Mesopotamia after several centuries of Akkadian and Gutian kings. It controlled the cities of Isin, Larsa and Eshnunna and extended as far north as the Jazira.

The Third Dynasty of Ur arose some time after the fall of the Akkad Dynasty. The period between the last powerful king of the Akkad Dynasty, Shar-kali-sharri, and the first king of Ur III, Ur-Nammu, is not well documented, but most Assyriologists posit that there was a brief "dark age", followed by a power struggle among the most powerful city-states... [Wik]

..

TRUE ETYMOLOGY

In addition to individual entries throughout the Mugsar, here we will start throwing in extra bits and pieces until we can get a feel for order...

Proto Language Monosyllables PLM

'Proto Language Monosyllables PLM with their Principal Meanings', Patrick C. Ryan ('2008) – "The Proto-Language was composed of 90 monosyllables..."

Some quite interesting points on true etymology and evolution.

Also notes "...one of the defining characteristics of *Emesal* is to eliminate from the 'female language' those sounds which would necessitate observable lip-rounding, presumably for whatever social significance observed lip-rounding by females may have had. *Emegi* [EG] **u** => *Emesal* [ES] **i** ..."

PIE = Proto-Indo-European

Refers often to **Kurt Jaritz** *Schriftarchäologie der altmesopotamischen Kultur* ('1967)

Ancient Signs: The Alphabet & the Origins of Writing - Andis Kaulins cites importance of Ryan's work - in addition to above: Sumerian Archaic Sign Table, Sumerian Sign Value Register
http://lingwhizt.blogspot.com/2011/01/8-origins-of-writing-in-western.html
- -
Some extracts from LINGUIST List 7.1247 involving Patrick C Ryan
http://linguistlist.org/issues/7/7-1247.html

..
Message 3: Sumerian and PIE
Date: Thu, 05 Sep 1996 01:10:28 EDT
From: Alan Huffman <aahny@cunyvm.cuny.edu>
Subject: Sumerian and PIE
Here are a couple more for your Sumerian / PIE list:
Sum.: me => 'I' [see copula note]
Sum.: adda => 'father' cf. Gothic atta
Sum.: nu => 'no'
Sum.: lugal => 'king' cf. Latin leg-is [and lu/ru interchangeability => rugal

=> English 'regal' - see note for entry at 12217 LUGAL]
..

Other Examples

ABZU = abyss :

1236A 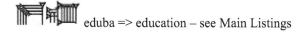 ZU = know

1200A ⬚ AB = cosmic sea, window

⬚ 1236A ZU, su_2 + 1200A AB = ABZU [reversed]

..

⬚ eduba => education – see Main Listings

..

122E7 ⬚ SUM, ŠUM$_2$, SI$_3$ => give cf. English 'to sum' total / add up; Greek 'sigma'

..

Shekel => origin of Hebrew term for money re price of bushel of grain, see 122BA SHE

Major Cities

Uruk / Sumerian: UNUG / cuneiform ^{URU} UNUG

12337 + 12014
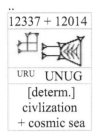
^{URU} UNUG
[determ.]
civlization
+ cosmic sea

Eridu / Sumerian eridu^{ki} / cuneiform NUN.KI

12263 + 121A0
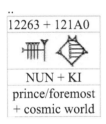
NUN + KI
prince/foremost
+ cosmic world

Ur / Sumerian URIM

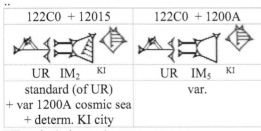

122C0 + 12015	122C0 + 1200A
UR IM$_2$ ^{KI}	UR IM$_5$ ^{KI}
standard (of UR) + var 1200A cosmic sea + determ. KI city	var.

UR, urin (uri$_3$, uru$_3$)
The name of the city is in origin derived from the god's name, URIM$_2$^{KI} being the classical Sumerian spelling of LAK-32.UNUG^{KI}, literally "the abode (UNUG) of Nanna (LAK-32)

APPENDIX

How to write on clay | Vowels | Syllabary | Copula | Foxvog's Basics

Abbreviations / Notations

[740x] = number of times attested – as noted by ePSD – it's important to note that a number of the signs (esp the hundreds of repetitive variants) in the standard lists were rarely used.

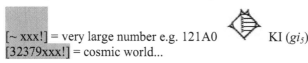

[~ xxx!] = very large number e.g. 121A0   KI (*gi₅*)
[32379xxx!] = cosmic world...

uQQ = unicode query – number?

gunû and šeššig

One method of generating new signs was to mark a portion of a base sign to specify the object intended. The marks are called by the scribes either gunû-strokes (from Sumerian gùn-a 'colored, decorated') or šeššig- hatchings (due to the resemblance of the strokes to the early cross-hatched form of the Sumerian sign for grain, še). Compare the following two sets of signs:

SAĜ	KA
DA	Á

   In the first set, the base sign is saĝ 'head'. Strokes over the mouth portion produces SAĜ-gunû, to be read ka 'mouth'. In the second set, the base sign is da 'side' (i.e., a shoulder, arm and hand). Hatchings over the arm portion produces DA-šeššig, to be read á 'arm'...
[Foxvog]

CVVE = compound verb verbal element (PSD)

PLM = Proto Language Monosyllables (see True Etym.)

How to write on clay

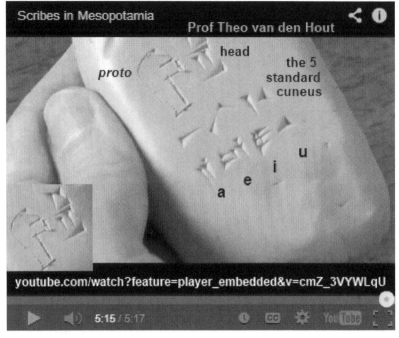

Professor Theo van den Hout:
youtube.com/watch?feature=player_embedded&v=cmZ_3VYWLqU

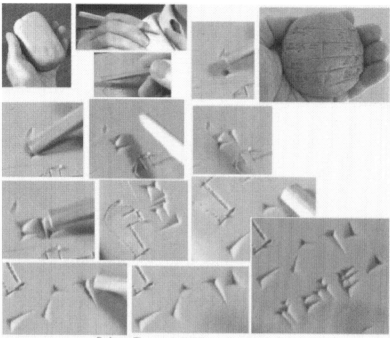

Professor Theo van den Hout
http://www.youtube.com/watch?feature=player_embedded&v=cmZ_3VYWLqU

Also carolineludovici.com/learn-how-to-write-cuneiform.html |

youtube.com/watch?feature=player_embedded&v=eJYQ8VEFznU

archaeology.otterlabs.org/Courses/AncientCivilizations/Syllabus/CuneiformLab.htm

Basic Cuneus

GE = stylus cuneus; (piece of) writing, copy, exemplar, written; blow; wound
[All called 'ge' but then 12100 reed (stylus) is also 'ge']

1230B ◁ ge_{14}

12038 ▻— ge_{15}

12079 ▼ ge_3

1203A ↖ ge_{22}

12039 ↘ ge_{23}

..

122B9 ●

Numbers

12038 ▷— ASH "1"

122F0 ⊨ MIN "2" (TAB)

1203C ⊨ ESH "3"

121F9 ⊨ LIMMU "4"

1213F ⊨ IA "5" [I vowel]

1240B 𒐋 ASH "6"

12153 𒅓 IMIN (5+2) "7"

1240D 𒐍 USSU "8"

12446 𒑆 ILIMMU (5+4) "9"

1230B ◁ U "10"

..

cpd 𒄑𒆪𒌋𒌋𒐀𒂍 geštu, ge-eš-tu = 60 (or 600?) [12100 gi confirm, designation, quality + 1230D eš 30 + 12305 tu small]

1214A 𒅊 IGI *gunû*, SIG$_7$ = 10000

Vowels

12000 𒀀 **A** (water)

1208A 𒂊 **E** (speak)

1213F 𒐊 **I** (5)

1230B 𒌋 **U** (10)

..

Pronunciation

Vowels may be pronounced as follows:
a - as in father,
e - as in peg,
i - as in hip,
u - as in pull.

Of the special consonants,

ñ is pronounced like 'ng' in rang, so **saĝ** would be *sang*,

ḫ is pronounced like 'ch' in German Buch (*bookkk*) or Scottish loch
(*lookkk*, not lock! ['x (ḫ)' h-breve plain velar fricative cf. (voiceless)
velar fricative /ḫ/ (sometimes just written h); Anatolian ḫ]) – tongue
slightly to roof of mouth and breathe through /out, throaty sound, like
something stuck in throat, bringing up phlegm] and š is pronounced like
'sh' in dash.

..

a, e₄: n., water; watercourse, canal; seminal fluid; offspring; father;
tears; flood.

é: house, household; temple; plot of land.

i: n., cry of pain (derived from ér, ir, 'tears; complaint' ?).

    v., to capture, defeat, overcome (cf., éd, è; i, 'to sprout')

ú: n., plant; vegetable; grass; food; bread; pasture; load.

    v., to nourish, support.

    adj., strong, powerful (man).

SUMERIAN CUNEIFORM DICTIONARY

ù : n., sleep (cf., u_5). [according to S. Lieberman, u, ù, and u_4 were pronounced /o/]

v., to sleep.

$u_{(3,4,8)}$: n., an expression of protest; cries, screams; the grunting, panting.

v., to bend over.

u_5 : n., male bird, cock; totality; earth pile or levee; raised area (sometimes written ù).

v., to mount (mating); to be on top of; to ride; to steer, conduct.

adj., (raised) high, especially land or ground (sometimes written ù).

u_{18} : huge.

u_{20} : barley.

More at sumerian.org/prot-sum – The Proto-Sumerian Language Invention Process - John A. Halloran

..

We do not know how Sumerian was spoken. Scribes were trained for over two years to become competent in Sumerian, the basis of the cuneiform writing system. The Sumerian cuneiform writing system consists of around 700 signs, which could represent both words and syllables. We must learn the language *as well as* the way it was written. Cuneiform is full of mysteries; it became increasingly complex over the three thousand years of its development, and its adepts utilized these complexities for esoteric teaching and speculation. While we cannot hope to duplicate the training or the native knowledge of the scribes, we must try in some way to make their teaching our own. We must begin by saying what they said, pronouncing what they pronounced. Although we cannot be certain how the languages were spoken, there are three ways to reconstruct pronunciation:

1. Comparing contemporary descended or related languages

2. Ancient transliterations or phonological discussions from the unknown to a known language

3. Borrowings from the unknown to a known language

Sumerian has no known descendants or relatives, so we must rely entirely on point number 2. Sumerian was written with the same set of characters, and for 2000 years... We work from the pronunciation of Akkadian back to the Sumerian. Finally, we are fairly confident of the *quality* of Sumerian vowels - whether it is an a, e, i, u (even perhaps o) - we have very little idea of the *quantity* - long or short, high or low, etc.

The following guide to Sumerian is therefore purely practical:

a short as in "bat," or long as in "father"

â long as in "father"

b as in "babble"

d as in English

e short as in "bet"

e sometimes long as in "day"

g hard as in English "gag"

ĝ nasal "ng" as in "thing"

ḫ rough [throaty] "h", no English equivalent

i short as in "sit"

i sometimes long as in "ski"

k always hard as in "kick"

l as in English

m same as English

n same as English

p same as English

r same as English, can be flat or rolled

s same as English

š like "sh" in "ship"

t as in English

u short as in "cut"

u sometimes long as in "ruby"

z as in English

There are two diphthongs:
"ia" pronounced "ee-yah" or "ya"
"ai" pronounced "ah-ee" or like the word "aye"
If any other two vowels come together, pronounce them like they are
both the first vowel.

(more: angelfire.com/tx/tintirbabylon/pron.html)

Syllabary A-Z: Write your name in cuneiform!

There's no 'o' vowel in Sumerian but 'u' (pron. as in pull) is close. Also use the Main Listings for 3-letter syllables like we did for Hogan

CV consonant vowel Ba

	a	e	i	u
	a 12000 water *á* A$_2$ 12009 arm	*e* 1208A *é* 1208D house	*i* 1213F 5 (five) *í* IÁ =5 1213F	*u* 1230B 10, hole *ú* 12311 food *ù* 12147 sleep
b	*ba* 12040 divide *bá*=PA 1227A beat *bà*=EŠ 12365 flour	*be*=BAD 12041 open *bé*=BI 12049 beer *bè*=NI 1224C oil/time	*bi* 12049 beer *bí*=NE 12248 fire *bì*=PI 1227F ear	*bu* 1204D long *bú*=KASKAL 1219C distance *bù*=PÙ 12164 mouth
d	*da* 12055 line *dá*=TA	*de*=DI 12072 justice *dè*=NE 12248 fire	*di* 12072 justice *dí*=TÍ	*du* 1207A go/come *dú*=TU 12305 dove

	122EB from [Syll. top]	[same bí]	1212D good	dù=GAG 12195 build du₄=TUM 12308 cross-beam
g	ga 120B5 carry/suckling gá 120B7 basket	ge=GI 12100 reed stylus gé=KID 121A4 field gè=DIŠ 12079 "1" one	gi 12100 reed stylus gí=KID 121A4 field gì=DIŠ 12079 "1" one gi₄ 12104 turn gi₅=KI 121A0 cosmic	gu 12116 cord gú 12118 neck gù=KA 12157 mouth/speak gu₄ 1211E bull gu₅=KU 121AA sit gu₆=NAG 12158 drink gu₇ 12165 eat
ḫ	ḫa 12129 fish ḫá=ḪI.A ḫa=U	ḫe=ḪI 1212D good ḫé=GAN	ḫi 1212D good ḫí=GAN	ḫu 12137 bird

	1230B 10, hole *ha₄*=ḪI 1212D good	120F6 bear young	120F6 bear young	
k	*ka* 12157 mouth/speak *ká* 1218D gate *kà*=GA 120B5 carry/suckling	*ke*=KI 121A0 cosmic *ké*=GI 12100 reed stylus	*ki*=KI 121A0 cosmic *kí*=GI 12100 reed stylus	*ku* 121AA sit *kú*=GU₇ 12165 eat *kù* 121AC pure *ku₄* 121AD enter
l	*la* 121B7 hang *lá*=LAL 121F2 small *là*=NU 12261 not	*le*=LI 121F7 bathe *lé*=NI 1224C oil/time	*li* 121F7 bathe *lí*=NI 1224C oil/time	*lu* 121FB sheep *lú* 121FD male
m	*ma* 12220 land	*me* 12228 copula *mé*=MI	*mi* 1222A black *mí*=MUNUS	*mu* 1222C year

má 12223 ship	1222A black *mè* / 1201E battle, copula / 12160	122A9 cuneus *mì*=ME 12228 copula	*mú*=SAR 122AC write
n *na* 1223E incense *ná* 1223F lay *nà*=AG 1201D do *na₄* ("NI.UD") 1224C oil/time + 12313 sun	*ne* 12248 carry / fire *né*=NI 1224C oil/time	*ni* 1224C oil/time *ní*=IM 1224E clay	*nu* 12261 not *nú*=NÁ 1223F lay
p *pa* 1227A foreman *pá*=BA [12400] "2"	*pe*=PI 1227F ear / intelligence *pé*=BI 12049 much, beer	*pi* 1227F ear *pí*=BI 12049 much, beer *pì*=BAD	*pu*=BU 1204D long *pú*=TÚL 121E5 source, well *pù*

SUMERIAN CUNEIFORM DICTIONARY

		12041 open	12164 mouth
r	*ra* 1228F beat *rá*=DU 1207A go/come	*re*=RI 12291 place *ré*=URU 12337 civilization	*ri* 12291 place *ri*=URU 12337 civilization	*ru* 12292 fall *rú*=GAG 12195 build *rù*=AŠ 12038 "1"
s	*sa* 12293 muscle *sá*=DI 12072 equal *sà*=ZA 1235D "4" *sa₄* ("ḪU.NÁ") 12137 bird + 1223E incense	*se*=SI 122DB horn *sé*=ZI 12363 life [Syll. top]	*si* 122DB horn *sí*=ZI 12363 life	*su* 122E2 skin, organ *sú*=ZU 1236A know *sù*=SUD 122E4 pull *su₄* uQQ red/brown
š	*ša* 122AD heart *šá*=NÍG uQQ [numeric??] *šà* 122AE heart	*še* 122BA barley *šé*, *šè* 12365 flour	*ši*=IGI 12146 eye *ší*=SI 122DB horn	*šu* 122D7 hand *šú* 122D9 ?? *šù*=ŠÈ 12365 flour

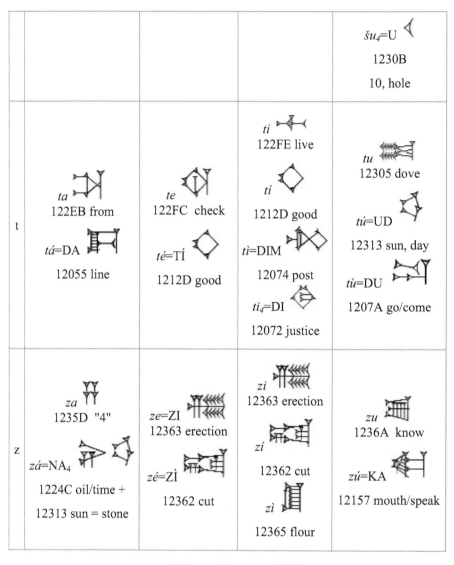

				$šu_4$=U 1230B 10, hole
t	*ta* 122EB from *tá*=DA 12055 line	*te* 122FC check *té*=TÍ 1212D good	*ti* 122FE live *tí* 1212D good *tì*=DIM 12074 post ti_4=DI 12072 justice	*tu* 12305 dove *tú*=UD 12313 sun, day *tù*=DU 1207A go/come
z	*za* 1235D "4" *zá*=NA₄ 1224C oil/time + 12313 sun = stone	*ze*=ZI 12363 erection *zé*=ZÌ 12362 cut	*zi* 12363 erection *zí* 12362 cut *zì* 12365 flour	*zu* 1236A know *zú*=KA 12157 mouth/speak

VC vowel consonant aB

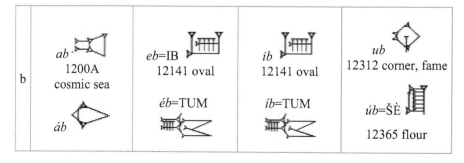

b	*ab* 1200A cosmic sea *áb*	*eb*=IB 12141 oval *éb*=TUM	*ib* 12141 oval *íb*=TUM	*ub* 12312 corner, fame *úb*=ŠÈ 12365 flour

	12016 cow	12308 cross-beam	12308 cross-beam	
d	*ad* 1201C father *ád* 12109 terror	*ed*=Á 12009 arm	*id*=Á 12009 palm *íd*=A.ENGUR 12000 water + 121C9 cosmic	*ud* 12313 sun *úd*=ÁŠ 1203E curse
g	*ag* 1201D do *ág* 12258 love	*eg*=IG 12145 door *ég*=E 1208A "vowel"	*ig* 12145 door *íg*=E 1208A "vowel"	*ug* 1228C tiger [Syll. top]
ḫ	*aḫ* 12134 *áḫ*=ŠEŠ 122C0 brother, assistant	*eḫ*=AḪ 12134	*iḫ*=AḪ 12134	*uḫ*=AḪ 12134 *uḫ* 12314 weathervane??
k	*ak*=AG 1201D do	*ek*=IG 12145 door	*ik*=IG 12145 door	*uk*=UG 1228C tiger

l	*al* 12020 hoe *ál*=ALAM 12029 statue, icon	*el* 12096 pure *él*=IL 1214B fish??	*il* 1214B fish?? *il* 1214D raise	*ul* 1230C *úl*=NU 12261 not
m	*am* **/** 12120 wild bull / 12094 'Eden' *ám*=ÁG 12258 love	*em*=IM 1214E tablet	*im* 1214E tablet *ím*=KAŠ₄ 1207D run	*um* 1231D reed rope *úm*= 12313 sun
n	*an* 1202D sky god [*Syll. top*	*QF*]	*en* 12097 lord *én*, *èn*=LI 121F7 bathe	*in* 12154 abuse *in₄*=EN 12097 lord *in₅*=NIN 122A9 cuneus + 12306 garment = lady, mistress	*un* 12326 people *ún*=U 1230B 10, hole

p	*ap*=AB 1200A cosmic sea	*ep*=IB 12141 oval *ép*=TUM 12308 cross-beam	*ip*=IB 12141 oval *ip*=TUM 12308 cross-beam	*up*=UB 12312 corner *úp*=ŠÈ 12365 flour
r	*ar* 12148 *ár*=UB 12312 corner	*er*=IR 12155 ask	*ir* 12155 ask *ip*=A.IGI 12000 water + 12146 eye	*ur* 12328 dog *úr* 1232B phallus
s	*as*=AZ 1228D bear	*es*=GIŠ 12111 tree *és*=EŠ 12365 flour	*is*=GIŠ 12111 tree *ís*=EŠ 12365 flour	*us*=UZ *ús*=UŠ 12351 male
š	*aš* 12038 one *áš* 1203E curse	*eš* 1230D "30" / 12401 eš$_6$ "3" *éš*=ŠÈ 12365 flour	*iš* 12156 mountain, summer *íš*=KASKAL 1219C distance	*uš* 12351 male *úš* = BAD die cf. open

t	*at*=AD 1201C father *át*=GÍR *gunû* 12109 knife??	*et*=Á A2 (kappu) 12009 palm, hand	*it*=Á A2 (kappu) 12009 palm, hand	*ut*=UD 12313 sun *út*=ÁŠ 1203E curse
z	*az* 1228D bear	*ez*=GIŠ 12111 tree *éz*=EŠ 12365 flour	*iz*= GIŠ 12111 tree *íz*=IŠ 12156 official	*uz* uQQ *úz*=UŠ 12351 male *ùz* 1235A goat

[END]

..

The tables above show signs used for simple syllables of the form CV or VC. As used for the Sumerian language, the cuneiform script was in principle capable of distinguishing at least 16 consonants, transliterated as

$$b, d, g, \tilde{g}, \underline{h}, k, l, m, n, p, r, \check{r}, s, š, t, z$$

as well as four vowel qualities: *a, e, i, u.* ...[Wik]

..

The picture of a hand came to stand not only for Sumerian šu ("hand") but also for the phonetic syllable šu in any required context. Sumerian words were largely monosyllabic, so the signs generally denoted syllables, and the resulting mixture is termed a word-syllabic script. The inventory of phonetic symbols henceforth enabled the Sumerians to denote grammatical elements by phonetic complements added to the word signs (logograms or ideograms). Because Sumerian had many identical sounding (homophonous) words, several logograms frequently yielded identical phonetic values and are distinguished in modern transliteration—(as, for example, **ba, bá, bà,** ba4). Because a logogram often represented several related notions with different names (e.g., "sun," "day," "bright"), it was capable of assuming more than one phonetic value (this feature is called polyphony)...more:everyhistory.org/1a-cuneiform1.html

..

...'accents' and subscript numerals do not affect the pronunciation – Halloran: sumerian.org/sumerlex.htm

..

Foxvog's Basics / Grammar

home.comcast.net/~foxvog/Grammar.pdf

Introduction to Sumerian Grammar pdf – Daniel **Foxvog**. At least at the beginning, shows the logograms too!

Sign Diacritics and Index Numbers

Sumerian features a large number of homonyms — words that were pronounced similarly but had different meanings and were written with different signs,

for example:

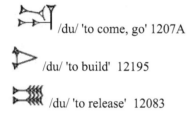

/du/ 'to come, go' 1207A

/du/ 'to build' 12195

/du/ 'to release' 12083

A system of numerical subscripts, and diacritics over vowels representing subscripts, serves to identify precisely which sign appears in the actual text Borger's index system which is used here is as follows:

Single-syllable signs	Multiple-syllable signs
du (= du₁)	muru
dú (= du₂)	múru
dù (= du₃)	mùru
du₄ etc.	muru₄

Note that the diacritic always falls on the first vowel of the word!

There is variation in the systems employed in older signlists for multiple- syllable signs, especially in Labat. In the earliest editions of his sign-list which may still be encountered in libraries, Labat carried the use of diacritics through index numbers 4-5 by shifting the acute and grave accents onto the first syllable of multiple-syllable signs:

murú (= muru$_2$)

murù (= muru$_3$)

múru (= muru$_4$)

mùru (= muru$_5$)

New values of signs, pronunciations for which no generally accepted index numbers yet exist, are given an "x" subscript, e.g. dax 'side'...

Many signs are polyvalent, that is, they have more than one value or reading...

...

Polyvalency

The most important new development by far was the principle of polyvalency, the association of "many values" with a particular sign, each with its own separate pronunciation. This became a very productive and simple method of generating new logographic values.

```
apin  'plow'    can also be read    uru₄    'to plow'
                                    engar   'plowman,  farmer'
                                    àbsin   'furrow'
```

Determinatives

To help the reader decide which possible value of a polyvalent sign was intended by the writer, the use of determinatives arose. A determinative is one of a limited number of signs which, when placed before or after a sign or group of signs, indicates that the determined object belongs to a particular semantic category, e.g. wooden, reed, copper or bronze objects, or persons, deities, places, etc. Determinatives were still basically optional as late as the Ur III period (7887-7997CT). When Sumerian died as a spoken language, they became obligatory. Determinatives were presumably not to be pronounced when a text was read, and to show that they are not actually part of a word we transliterate them, in unilingual Sumerian context at least, as superscripts. To use the example of the 'plow' sign above, the polyvalent sign APIN [see 12033] is read

APIN - if preceded by a 'wood' determinative: GIŠAPIN 'plow'

ENGAR - if preceded by a 'person' determinative: LÚENGAR 'plowman'

but URU$_4$ 'to plow' or ÀBSIN 'furrow' elsewhere, depending upon context.

Rebus Writing and Syllabic Values

At some point rebus writings arose, where the sign for an object which could easily be drawn was used to write a homophonous word which could not so easily be depicted, especially an abstract idea. For example, the picture of an arrow, pronounced /ti/, became also the standard sign for ti 'rib' as well as for the verb ti(l) 'to live'. The adoption of the rebus principle was a great innova- tion, but it adds to the difficulty of learning the Sumerian writing system, since meanings of words thus written are divorced entirely from the original basic shapes and meanings of their signs.

...The Sumerian writing system was still in limited use as late as the [100ᵗʰ] cent.; the last known texts are astronomical in nature and can be dated to ca. [10076CT]. The system thus served the needs of Mesopotamian civilizations for a continuous span of over 3200 years – a remarkable achievement in human history.

Syllabic Signs

Used in Sumerian primarily to write grammatical elements. They are also commonly used to write words for which there is no proper logogram. Sometimes this phonetic writing is a clue that the word in question is a foreign loanword.

1) The sign ĝeštug is written: PI

2) The sign ĝéštug is written: ĝeš-túgPI

3) The sign ĝèštug is written: ĝešPItúg

Determinatives

Logograms which may appear before or after words which categorize the latter in a variety of ways. They are orthographic aids and were presumably not pronounced in actual speech. They begin to be used spora- dically by the end of the archaic period. While they were probably developed to help a reader chose the desired value of a polyvalent sign, they are often employed obligatorily even when the determined logogram is not polyvalent. For example, while the wood determinative ĝiš may be used before the PA sign to help specify its reading ĝidri 'scepter', rather than, e.g., sìg 'to beat', ĝiš is also used before hašhur 'apple (tree or wood)' even though this sign has no other reading. Other common functions are to help the reader distinguish between homonymous words, e.g. ad 'sound' and ᵍⁱˢAD 'plank' or between different related meanings of a word, e.g. nú 'to sleep' but ᵍⁱˢĝèšnu (NÚ) 'bed'. The following determinatives are placed BEFORE the words they determine and so are referred to as pre-determinatives:

Determinative	Meaning	Category
I (abbr. [m])	one, (item)	personal names (usually male)
lú	man, person	male professions
munus (abbr. [f])	woman, female	female names and professions*
diĝir (abbr. [d])	god	deities
dug	pot	vessels
gi	reed	reed varieties and objects
ĝiš	tree, wood	trees, woods and wooden objects
i₇ (or íd)	watercourse	canals and rivers
kuš	skin	leather hides and objects
mul	star	planets, stars and constellations
na₄	stone	stones and stone objects
šim	aromatic, resin	aromatic substances
túg (or tu₉)	garment	(woolen) garments
ú	grass	grassy plants, herbs, cereals
iri	city	city names (previously read uru)
urudu	copper	copper (and bronze) objects
uzu	flesh	body parts, meat cuts

The following determinatives are placed AFTER the words they determine and so are referred to as post-determinatives:

ki	place	cities and other geographic entities
ku₆	fish	fish, amphibians, crustaceans
mušen	bird	birds, insects, other winged animals
nisi(g)	greens	vegetables (the obsolete reading sar 'garden plot' is still also seen)
zabar	bronze	bronze objects (often combined with the pre-determinative urudu)

Sumerian Grammar '2003 (Internet Archive) – Dietz Otto Edzard
archive.org/details/SumerianGrammarhdo
..

uCode query

 a-a (aya) [561x] = father

 SU$_4$, SI$_4$ [184x] = to be red brown

 KUSHU / KUŠU, kuš$_2$ [149x] = tired, troubled | cpd
kuš$_2$-a-ni-ta = to be tired

uQQ kuš$_2$ tired + 12000 A cry of woe + 1224C NI come to an end + 122EB TA
much

 šá=NÍG [syllabary]

 peš [67x] thick; give birth - see 12912

Copula

I$_3$- am$_3$-me

to be

1224C	cpd	12228
I$_3$	am$_3$	me
time, comes to pass	aux. 12000 A progeny + 1202D deity	to be, is

http://etcsl.orinst.ox...c625.15.3...

also

1214E
em
to be

psd.museum.upenn.edu/epsd/epsd/e3660.html

..

[More *True Etym.* English "I", "am", "me"!]

Tablet Examples

Gilgamesh Flood Tablet
(cdli.ox.ac.uk/wiki/doku.php?id=objects1to10)

Ur-Nammu [7954-7971CT] founded the Sumerian 3rd dynasty of Ur, in southern Mesopotamia, following several centuries of Akkadian and Gutian rule... chiefly remembered today for his legal code, The Code of Ur-Nammu, the oldest known law code surviving today. It is written on tablets, in the Sumerian language [c.7900CT]....[Wik]

Ur-Nammu Law Code oldest laws known Sumer 7900CT
(300 years before Hammurabi code)

schoyencollection.com/music.html (MS 2064)

Earliest record musical instruments 23 types listed
Sumer 7400CT
schoyencollection.com/music.html (MS 2340)

Considering the extent to which Sumerians invent musical
instruments and writing about music, makes you wonder when you
look at cuneiform like ⊞ (12156 kuš₇ civil servant) about the true
origins of the music staff and notes layout ♪ [and the bullet
point!]

..

Letter to a sister complaining about
her stinginess (Lutz 1917 no 15)

[Cuneiform Texts and the Writing of History
- Marc Van De Mieroop - more:
books.google.com]

Project Home Invitation

PROJECT HOME INVITATION

| True Edu. Founders | True Year Dating | True Mateship | True Shakespeare |
| Sumerians not Greeks | CT not religio | BILLJIM not Bill | Vere not Shaxper |

(australiansofarabia.wordpress.com)

THE D.A.P. SCORE - *The Impostor Exposor Calculator*

D x A x P = score

We have all these famous people. But how can we be sure they deserve
the credit. "History is full of dead white males". Often privileged with
lots of family money and connections, one's father was even 'god'. The
ones that weren't so privileged were supposed to be natural geniuses –
but a closer look shows that there is very little concrete historical
evidence to support what they have supposed to have done – myth
becomes fact, history re-written. There really is no need to separate a
Library into *Fiction* and *Non-Fiction* – it's all *Fiction*. All this
spinmeistering is to suit some group's purpose, and usually becomes an
established powerful money making industry, including *Will Extortion* of
the gullible elderly, the *"Tickets to Heaven"* con job – leaving future
generations dispossessed and invariably lined up at Centrelink.

The "D.A.P. Score" is a formula for ranking people – an imposter
exposer calculator, if you like. It is designed to weed out famous,
influential people who have had a lot of help, to say the least. Each of the
3 variables has a maximum score of 10. So the total maximum score is
1000.

You can calculate the DAP score for anybody, yourself or some famous
figure.

"**D**" = Degree of DIFFICULTY – in getting started / growing up, e.g.
born into a 3rd world or advanced nation, poor or affluent family, well-
grounded/stable or dysfunctional upbringing – alcoholic or caring
parents, etc.
So a very difficult start would score near 10, a very easy start, lots of
assistance from family, connections, stable advanced economy would
score near 0.
Remember that if "D" is low or zero, there's not much point in
continuing further and analyzing the next variables "A" and "P" –
because even if they are maximums you still end up with zilch: 0 x 10 x
10 = 0

"**A**" = Degree of ACHIEVEMENT based on "D" (the degree of difficulty
in getting started).

"**P**" = Degree of POTENTIAL, essentially for 'immortality'.

Thus, in summary, DAP = D x A x P

The maximum is 10 x 10 x 10 = 1000

Let's now look at some examples:

* William Shakspere

William Shakspere (seems to have been spelt lots of different ways – we only have 6 dubious signatures - no letters or manuscripts, because he was likely illiterate) - held out to be *William Shakespeare,*the playwright, by the multi-billion dollar Stratford industry. *Degree of Difficulty* pretty average, didn't achieve anything above the ordinary, but has a strong potential for immortality. Yep, the *Establishment* has credited him with the achievements of *Edward de Vere.* Just shows you if they can get away with re-writing history in this case, what else do they teach our children that has no sound foundation in a little thing called 'reality'.

William Shakspere's – most likely pronounced 'shack' or 'shax' - de Vere used the name *William Shake-speare* (it was often hyphenated as an extra clue for the *coneys*) because of the similarity to the *Pallas Athena* goddess of Wisdom motif of *shaking the spear* at ignorance) and it neatly coincided as part of his coat of arms as *Lord Bolbec* :

Guillem Shaxper's DAP score = 10 x 0 x 10 = 0 (0% of a maximum 1000)

* T.E. Lawrence

Probably blame Lowell Thomas (the American journalist commissioned by the government to get the wary public interested in sending their sons to the slaughter, he started out in the Western front stalemate, then had the bright idea to check out the Middle East campaign – and the first of several allied agents dressed in Arab costume that he saw … well, he could just see how it could be marketed).

Somewhat 'Difficult' start – father runs off with maid, takes her name, which really means Lawrence is 'Chapman' – finding out he was actually a bastard seems to have effected him; didn't 'Achieve' what Hollywood said he did – that was the Australian Light Horse; but he certainly does have the 'Potential' for immortality, if there's an industry making money out of the '*Myth as historical Fact*' market.

Ned's (that's what his family called him) DAP score = 5 x 0 x 10 = 0 (0% of a maximum 1000)

* Bill Gates

Has the strong potential to be the richest man that will ever live.

His "D" score: born into an advanced nation, affluent family line, and again, given the achievement bug by his grandmother.

A closer look at the development of Microsoft shows that it if not for, Paul Allen, Bill Gates would be still trying to graduate from Harvard. It was Allen that first identified the seed of the future Microsoft. And much of the later software, that fueled the exponential development was essentially plagiarized.

So again we have a "D" score approaching 0.

Thus, a rough 'prima facie' guess would throw up:

Bill Gate's DAP score = 0 x 10 x 10 = 0 (0% of a maximum 1000)

* Albert Einstein

The "D" score: born into an advanced nation, reasonably affluent family, considerable useful influence came from his uncle, excellent academic environment / facilities, and a first wife that may well have played a greater role than we will ever know.
The "A" and "P" scores are pretty obvious.

Thus, a rough 'prima facie' guess would throw up:

Albert Einstein's DAP score = 7 x 10 x 10 = 700 (70% of a maximum 1000)

* James Watson

James Watson along with Francis Crick and Maurice Wilkins shot to fame, including the '1962 Nobel Prize for their structure of DNA – the double helix, but they lifted the work of **Rosalind Franklin** (b. 25 July '1920).

She was the ultimate loser, dying of cancer at age 38 in '1958 (*talk about bad luck!*) never knowing just how much her colleagues ripped her off, because to them she was just a stupid female. The plagiarists basked in their sham glory past their 80s. Refer p563-8 *Science – A History*, John Gribbin, and the *"Rosalind Franklin – The Dark Lady of DNA"*, Brenda Maddox)

James Watson's DAP score = 0 x 0 x 10 = 0 (0% of a maximum 1000)

* * *

To finish on a positive note:

* Charles 'Hank' Bukowski
Bukowski had a shitty start, but stumbled on to John Martin, who himself commands a high DAP score. In a sense the two men are inextricably coupled for eternity.

Bukowski's DAP score = 10 x 10 x 10 = 1000 (100% of a maximum 1000)

* *"Billjim"*
This one is still being played out.

Billjim DAP score = 10 x 10 x ? = [remains to be seen - are plebs becoming empowered enough with the Internet?]

..

DAP Feedback:
From: Laurel Smith
ladydoconthebayou@earthlink.net
To: peter_hogan@hotmail.com [old email address]
Subject: DAP
Date: Fri, 05 May 2000 23:17:41 -0500
MIME-Version: 1.0
Received: from [207.217.121.50] by hotmail.com (3.2) with ESMTP
id MHotMailBADCE7830026D82197D0CFD979329D400; Fri May 05
21:16:04 2000
Received: from earthlink.net (1Cust227.tnt5.houma.la.da.uu.net
[63.14.152.227]) by avocet.prod.itd.earthlink.net (8.9.3/8.9.3) with
ESMTP id
VAA14700for ; Fri, 5 May 2000 21:16:01 -0700 (PDT)
From: ladydoconthebayou@earthlink.net
Fri May 05 21:16:23 2000
Message-ID: <39139CE5.C229E9C@earthlink.net>
X-Mailer: Mozilla 4.05 [en]C-NECCK (Win95; U)

I appreciate the concept. Very eloquently organized.

..

"The D.A.P. Score" was first developed by Peter Hogan in Shinsaibashi Japan '1993

Mugsar School Modules

Key student assignments:

⟩ How Sumerian Scribes were really thinking in those first schools 5,000 years ago by posting new Mugsar 4-Ways of famous texts and suggesting fresh, more poignant translations.

⟩ Conjure missing words / concepts in cuneiform, i.e. create new compounds especially for intellectual 'big words' and new technology terms.

..

Post your creations #MugsarSumerian #[Your School]

..

⟩ Mugsar International School Debating Competition - to be run by designated Mugsar Home School (australiansofarabia.wordpress.com) - cash prizes sponsored by major Mugsar Immortal Benefactors will provide significant school funding - the ineluctable question:

"What kind of a student is a student who does not know Sumerian?"

Mugsar Immortal Benefactor Register (MIBR)

The online MIBR is being developed at MugsarSumerian.com here.

Format example:

MIB No.:

12017CT02071441

[YearMonthDate Immortalized]

Family Name:

The Xxxxxx Family

Message in a Bottle:

Family Photo:

City/Town, Country:

Xxxxxx, Xxxxxx

Immortalized by:

Xxxxxx Xxxxxx

Mugsar Location:

Sign: 12000 A vowel water

Plus various other optional fields like Location links to plot: sign / compound / section – more details at online MIBR.

..

You know plain and simple, it's not just after you're gone, nobody knows you ever existed, it starts way before.

It ain't getting less competitive out there.

As a parent, what's something special that you can put on your kid's application to a top university like Harvard?

Parents' Occupation: "Nothing Special"

Family's Altruistic Activities: "Nothing Special"

Kid graduates one day from an average college with millions of others, what's something special to put on the resume?

Kid's Internships: "Nothing Special"

If I was a parent, my eyes would be lighting up on that empty starting MIBR list.

How would it look to have our family in the first 10, for all time, to boot.

A couple of grand to sponsor a sign, shoot, what have I got to lose ...what if this sucker takes off some day?

At any moment, you could be watching *Jimmy Fallon*, and the new game is

"Who can find the Mugsar sign the fastest?"

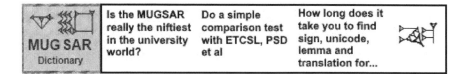

Or some rich eccentric might be smitten about stirring up the Establishment, and puts $50,000,000 straight into advertising for just one line on a screen:

"What kind of a student is a student who does not know Sumerian?"

Mugsar QuickFinder

1-2

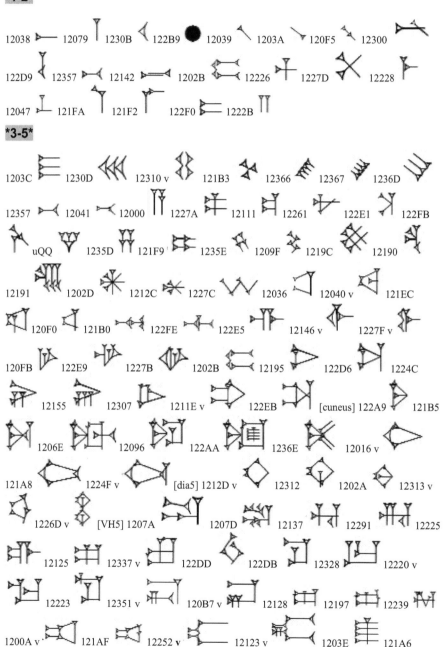

3-5

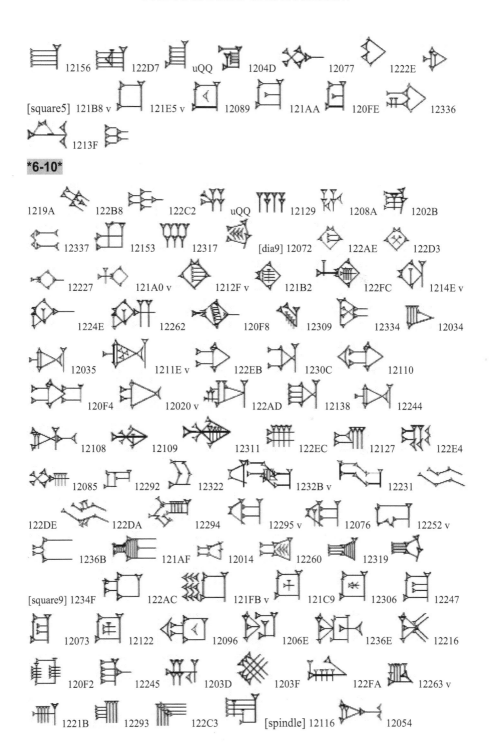

12156 122D7 uQQ 1204D 12077 1222E

[square5] 121B8 v 121E5 v 12089 121AA 120FE 12336

1213F

6-10

1219A 122B8 122C2 uQQ 12129 1208A 1202B

12337 12153 12317 [dia9] 12072 122AE 122D3

12227 121A0 v 1212F v 121B2 122FC 1214E v

1224E 12262 120F8 12309 12334 12034

12035 1211E v 122EB 1230C 12110

120F4 12020 v 122AD 12138 12244

12108 12109 12311 122EC 12127 122E4

12085 12292 12322 1232B v 12231

122DE 122DA 12294 12295 v 12076 12252 v

1236B 121AF 12014 12260 12319

[square9] 1234F 122AC 121FB v 121C9 12306 12247

12073 12122 12096 1206E 1236E 12216

120F2 12245 1203D 1203F 122FA 12263 v

1221B 12293 122C3 [spindle] 12116 12054

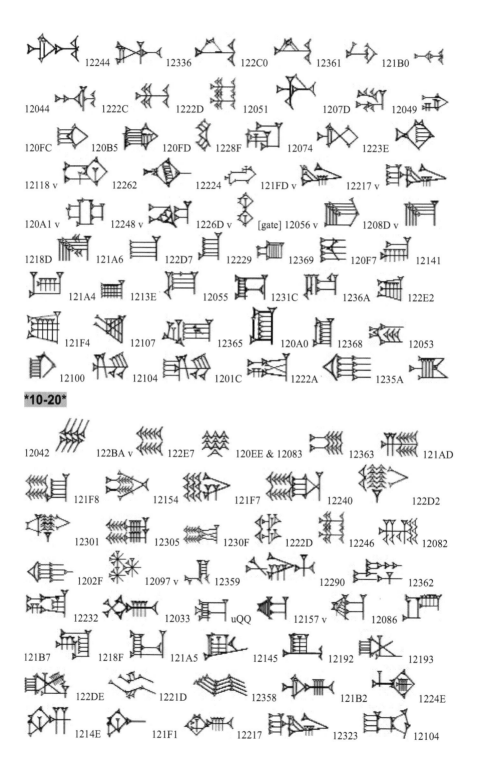

12244   12336   122C0   12361   121B0

12044   1222C   1222D   12051   1207D   12049

120FC   120B5   120FD   1228F   12074   1223E

12118 v   12262   12224   121FD v   12217 v

120A1 v   12248 v   1226D v   [gate] 12056 v   1208D v

1218D   121A6   122D7   12229   12369   120F7   12141

121A4   1213E   12055   1231C   1236A   122E2

121F4   12107   12365   120A0   12368   12053

12100   12104   1201C   1222A   1235A

10-20

12042   122BA v   122E7   120EE & 12083   12363   121AD

121F8   12154   121F7   12240   122D2

12301   12305   1230F   1222D   12246   12082

1202F   12097 v   12359   12290   12362

12232   12033   uQQ   12157 v   12086

121B7   1218F   121A5   12145   12192   12193

122DE   1221D   12358   121B2   1224E

1214E   121F1   12217   12323   12104

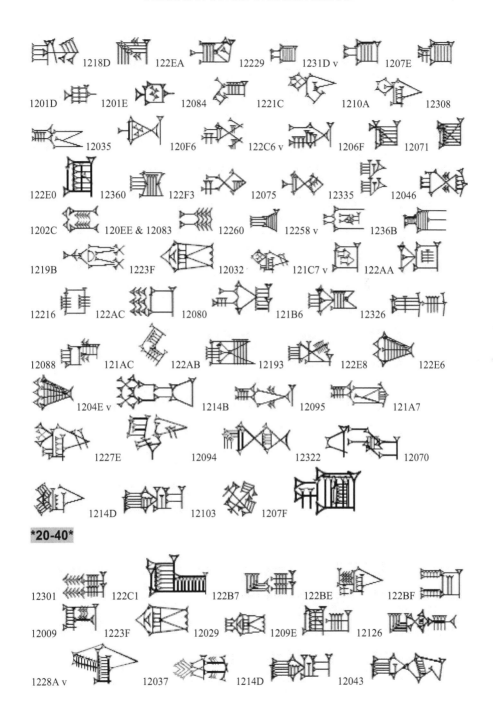

1218D 122EA 12229 1231D v 1207E

1201D 1201E 12084 1221C 1210A 12308

12035 120F6 122C6 v 1206F 12071

122E0 12360 122F3 12075 12335 12046

1202C 120EE & 12083 12260 12258 v 1236B

1219B 1223F 12032 121C7 v 122AA

12216 122AC 12080 121B6 12326

12088 121AC 122AB 12193 122E8 122E6

1204E v 1214B 12095 121A7

1227E 12094 12322 12070

1214D 12103 1207F

20-40

12301 122C1 122B7 122BE 122BF

12009 1223F 12029 1209E 12126

1228A v 12037 1214D 12043

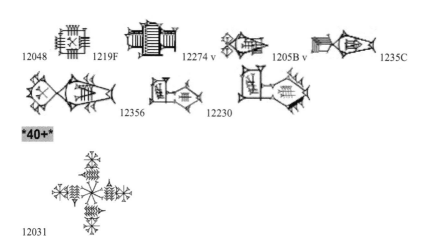

12048   1219F   12274 v   1205B v   1235C

12356   12230

40+

12031

QFNotes: Excl repetitive variants (base sign - usu on left) = **v**
duplicate where shapes are similar; 340 entries

..

Major Lemma

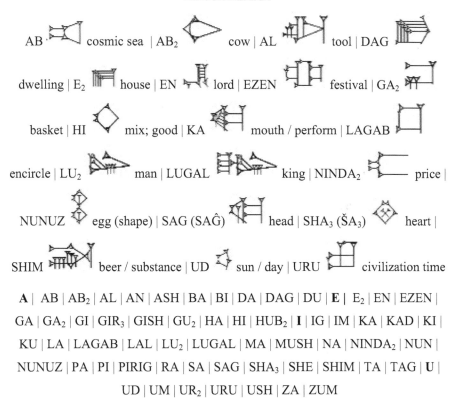

AB cosmic sea | AB₂ cow | AL tool | DAG dwelling | E₂ house | EN lord | EZEN festival | GA₂ basket | HI mix; good | KA mouth / perform | LAGAB encircle | LU₂ man | LUGAL king | NINDA₂ price | NUNUZ egg (shape) | SAG (SAĜ) head | SHA₃ (ŠA₃) heart | SHIM beer / substance | UD sun / day | URU civilization time

A | AB | AB₂ | AL | AN | ASH | BA | BI | DA | DAG | DU | **E** | E₂ | EN | EZEN | GA | GA₂ | GI | GIR₃ | GISH | GU₂ | HA | HI | HUB₂ | **I** | IG | IM | KA | KAD | KI | KU | LA | LAGAB | LAL | LU₂ | LUGAL | MA | MUSH | NA | NINDA₂ | NUN | NUNUZ | PA | PI | PIRIG | RA | SA | SAG | SHA₃ | SHE | SHIM | TA | TAG | **U** | UD | UM | UR₂ | URU | USH | ZA | ZUM

MUG SAR
Dictionary

Mugsar Sumerian
.com

We are in the
Immortality business!
we ride
Civilization Time
Forever

Peter Hogan
Mugsar Founder

amazonkindle

e: sumeriancuneiformdictionary
@gmail.com

+61 490 145 766

PO Box 1 Potts Pt NSW 1335 AU

ABN: 90 622 826 342

Mugsar Sumerian Cuneiform Dictionary

The only standalone dictionary in the world for the founders of Western Civilization and modern business 5,000 years ago.

Immortality For Sale

Get listed on the 'Mugsar Immortal Benefactors Register (MIBR)' by sponsoring a sign.

MugsarFest - Rockdale Workshops | Clay Tablets Tutoring | GameApp

amazonkindle

Mugsar Collector's Edition
(Pub. *Solstice* 21 June 12017 CT)
amazon.com/dp/B0732LFM7K
or search Amazon Kindle:
Education - Reference -
Sumerian Cuneiform Mugsar
Customized Edition
Direct purchase from Pete
- "Virtual Tablet In-scribe"

To check top Google ranking:
Google images
how to really impress someone

Mugsar Finder's Commission 80% !!!

First you have to be an existing MIB - for as little as $10 (which could come out of your commission) you could sponsor something on the Mugsar. You find a prospective MIB, email us and negotiate the price of a sign or section they will sponsor. It could be $1000+ You take 80% See home for more details.

Pete's Personal Tablet In-Scribe

To:

[Pete's inscribe to you on an early business card design draft with associated email could be worth a lot of money to a descendant one day - more so, if the original physical version follows - and even a Youtube video!]

Made in the USA
Las Vegas, NV
30 September 2021